MP3 파일 다운로드
www.kimoonsa.co.kr

호텔서비스사, 관광통역안내사, 항공사 승무원 시험대비

관광·호텔·항공 실무영어

배 상 정 저

TOURISM, HOTEL, AIRLINES
PRACTICAL ENGLISH

기문사
www.kimoonsa.co.kr

머리말 *Preface*

요즈음을 흔히 정보화 사회 또는 세계화 시대라고 부른다. 한 발자국이라도 앞서가려는 정보 전쟁이 치열하고 이 세계를 하나의 지구촌이라고 부를 만큼 외국을 이웃집 드나들듯 하는 추세에 부응하기 위해서는 국제 공용어(Common Language)인 영어로의 의사소통은 가히 필수적이라고 말해도 과언이 아닐 것이다.

이 책은 관광실무영어의 기본 용어부터 관광영어회화의 대화연습까지 다양한 상황으로 나뉘어져 있어 필요할 때마다 참조할 수 있도록 하였으며, 무엇보다도 관광가이드 및 해외여행을 계획하고 있는 사람들을 위한 회화공부, 그리고 관광 관련자격증을 준비하고 있는 사람들을 위한 수험교재가 되도록 노력하였다.

이 책의 구성은 다음과 같다.

1. Vocabulary and Patterns : 꼭 알아야 할 기본, 문형, 대화와 자격증시험에 출제되었던 어휘, 관광용어 및 면접 기출 문제
2. Patterns Drill : 여러 가지 다양한 문형 표현 훈련

3. Utterance-Response Drills : 상황에 따른 대화 연습

4. Dialogue : 여러 가지 다양한 대화 연습

5. Role Play : 한영, 영한 발화 연습

6. 호텔서비스사(관리사), 관광통역안내사, 항공사 승무원 시험 기출문제 및 예상문제(TOEIC. TOEFL L/C, R/C) 등으로 구성되어 있다.

아무쪼록 이 책이 관광실무영어를 공부하고 싶은 독자들의 소망에 조그마한 보탬이 되었으면 하는 바람이다.

2011. 1

저자 일동

차례 Contents

Unit 01

At the Airport

1 Vocabulary and Patterns

* disembarkation 입국카드 / embarkation card 출국카드 / visa 입국사증
  security processing 보안수속 / passport control 여권 심사대

* immigration office 이민국(출입국 사무소)
  immigration officer 이민국 직원(출입국 심사관)

* purpose of trip 여행목적

EX

A : What's the purpose of your trip?
B : (I'm here) for sightseeing.

* baggage, luggage 수화물 / extra weight 초과중량
  baggage claim tag 수하물표, 짐표 / suitcase 여행용 가방
  carry-on baggage 탑승 휴대물

EX

A : How many pieces of carry-on baggage do you have?
B : One.

* customs(house) 세관 / customs declaration 세관신고서
  customs officer 세관원
* quarantine office 검역소 / quarantine officer 검역관
* personal effects 일상 휴대품 / prohibited articles 휴대 금지품
* gifts 선물 / souvenirs 기념품
* date of birth(birth date) 생년월일

EX

A : What's your birth date?
B : May 18th, 1976. (공식 서류에는 day/mo/yr 순으로 표기하기도 함)

* signature of bearer 소지인의 서명
* nationality 국적

EX

A : What's your nationality?
B : Korea.

■ Landing Card(입국신고서) / Ⅰ-94 Form

미국 입국 신고서(비자 면제 대상 승객)

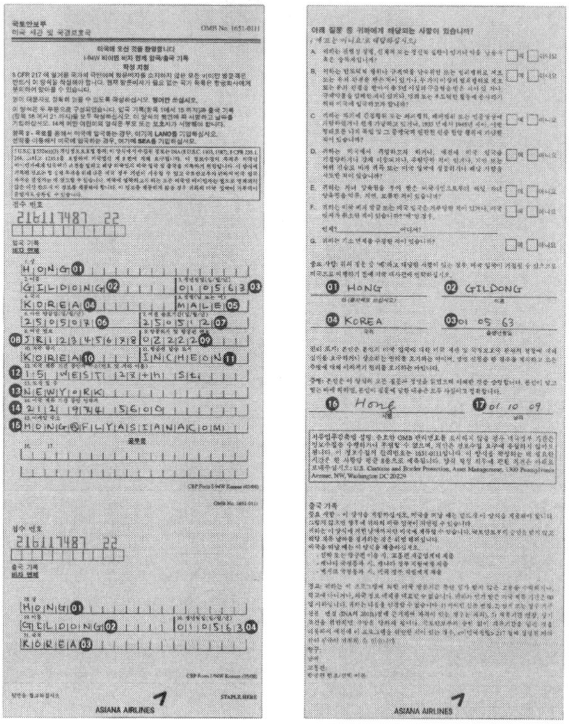

미국 입국 신고서(비자 소지 승객)

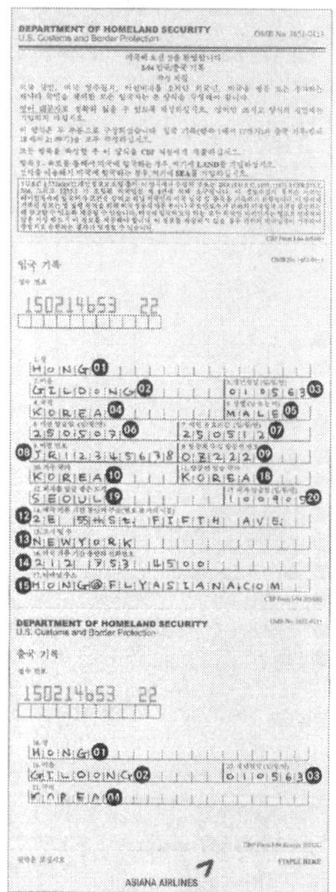

미국 출입국 카드 I-94의 구형 카드 사용이 종료됨에 따라, 지난 2009년 10월 1일부터 신형 카드로만 출입국 신고서를 작성하셔야 합니다. 신형 카드에는 여권 발급일과 유효기간, 미국 체류 기간 동안의 전화번호와 개인 이메일 주소 목록이 신설되었습니다.

- 01 성
- 02 이름
- 03 생년월일(일/월/년)
- 04 국적
- 05 성별(남/여)
- 06 여권 발급일
- 07 여권 유효기간
- 08 여권 번호
- 09 항공기 편명
- 10 거주국
- 11 항공편 탑승 도시
- 12 체제 기간 중 주소
- 13 주소지의 시 및 주
- 14 체류 기간 중 연락처
- 15 이메일 주소
- 16 서명
- 17 입국날짜
- 18 항공편 탑승 국가
- 19 비자 발행 도시
- 20 비자 발행 일자(일/월/년)

DEPARTMENT OF HOMELAND SECURITY
U.S. Customs and Border Protection — OMB No. 1651-0111

Admission Number — *Welcome to the United States*

390911988 18

I-94 Arrival/Departure Record - Instructions

This form must be completed by all persons except U.S. Citizens, returning resident aliens, aliens with immigrant visas, and Canadian Citizens visiting or in transit.

Type or print legibly with pen in ALL CAPITAL LETTERS. Use English. Do not write on the back of this form.

This form is in two parts. Please complete both the Arrival Record (Items 1 through 13) and the Departure Record (Items 14 through 17).

When all items are completed, present this form to the CBP Officer.

Item 7 - If you are entering the United States by land, enter **LAND** in this space. If you are entering the United States by ship, enter **SEA** in this space.

CBP Form I-94 (10/04)

Admission Number — OMB No. 1651-0111

390911988 18

Arrival Record

1. Family Name
2. First (Given) Name
3. Birth Date (Day/Mo/Yr)
4. Country of Citizenship
5. Sex (Male or Female)
6. Passport Number
7. Airline and Flight Number
8. Country Where You Live
9. City Where You Boarded
10. City Where Visa was Issued
11. Date Issued (Day/Mo/Yr)
12. Address While in the United States (Number and Street)
13. City and State

CBP Form I-94 (10/04)

Departure Number — OMB No. 1651-0111

390911988 18

I-94
Departure Record

14. Family Name
15. First (Given) Name
16. Birth Date (Day/Mo/Yr)
17. Country of Citizenship

CBP Form I-94 (10/04)

See Other Side — **STAPLE HERE**

This Side For Government Use Only

Primary Inspection

Applicant's Name ____________

Date Referred ________ Time ________ Insp. # ________

Reason Referred

☐ 212A ☐ ☐ ☐ PP ☐ Visa ☐ Parole ☐ SLB ☐ TWOV

☐ Other ____________

Secondary Inspection

End Secondary Time ________ Insp. # ________

Disposition ____________

18. Occupation	19. Waivers
20. CIS A Number **A -**	21. CIS FCO
22. Petition Number	23. Program Number
24. ☐ Bond	25. ☐ Prospective Student

26. Itinerary/Comments

27. TWOV Ticket Number

Warning A nonimmigrant who accepts unauthorized employment is subject to deportation.
Important - Retain this permit in your possession; ***you must surrender it when you leave the U.S.*** Failure to do so may delay your entry into the U.S. in the future. You are authorized to stay in the U.S. only until the date written on this form. To remain past this date, without permission from Department of Homeland Security authorities, is a violation of the law.
Surrender this permit when you leave the U.S.:
- By sea or air, to the transportation line;
- Across the Canadian border, to a Canadian Official;
- Across the Mexican border, to a U.S. Official.

Students planning to reenter the U.S. within 30 days to return to the same school, see "Arrival-Departure" on page 2 of Form I-20 **prior to surrendering this permit.**

Record of Changes

Port: — **Departure Record**
Date:
Carrier:
Flight # / Ship Name:

■ Customs Declaration(세관신고서)

U.S. Customs and Border Protection

Customs Declaration

19 CFR 122.27, 148.12, 148.13, 148.110,148.111, 1498; 31 CFR 5316

FORM APPROVED OMB NO. 1651-0009

Each arriving traveler or responsible family member must provide the following information (only ONE written declaration per family is required):

1. Family **Name**
   First *(Given)* Middle
2. **Birth date** Day Month Year
3. Number of **Family members** traveling with you
4. (a) U.S. Street **Address** (hotel name/destination)
   (b) City (c) State
5. **Passport issued by** (country)
6. **Passport number**
7. Country of **Residence**
8. **Countries visited** on this trip prior to U.S. arrival
9. **Airline/Flight No.** or **Vessel Name**
10. The primary purpose of this trip is **business**: Yes No
11. I am (We are) bringing
    (a) fruits, vegetables, plants, seeds, food, insects: Yes No
    (b) meats, animals, animal/wildlife products: Yes No
    (c) disease agents, cell cultures, snails: Yes No
    (d) soil or have been on a farm/ranch/pasture: Yes No
12. I have (We have) been in close proximity of (such as touching or handling) **livestock**: Yes No
13. I am (We are) carrying **currency or monetary instruments** over $10,000 U.S. or foreign equivalent: Yes No
    (see definition of monetary instruments on reverse)
14. I have (We have) **commercial merchandise**: Yes No
    (articles for sale, samples used for soliciting orders, or goods that are not considered personal effects)
15. **Residents** — the **total value of all goods**, including commercial merchandise I/we have purchased or acquired abroad, (including gifts for someone else, but not items mailed to the U.S.) and am/are bringing to the U.S. is: $
    Visitors — the **total value of all articles** that will remain in the U.S., including commercial merchandise is: $

Read the instructions on the back of this form. Space is provided to list all the items you must declare.

I HAVE READ THE IMPORTANT INFORMATION ON THE REVERSE SIDE OF THIS FORM AND HAVE MADE A TRUTHFUL DECLARATION.

X (Signature) Date (day/month/year)

For Official Use Only

CBP Form 6059B (10/07)

U.S. Customs and Border Protection Welcomes You to the United States

U.S. Customs and Border Protection is responsible for protecting the United States against the illegal importation of prohibited items. CBP officers have the authority to question you and to examine you and your personal property. If you are one of the travelers selected for an examination, you will be treated in a courteous, professional, and dignified manner. CBP Supervisors and Passenger Service Representatives are available to answer your questions. Comment cards are available to compliment or provide feedback.

Important Information

U.S. Residents — Declare all articles that you have acquired abroad and are bringing into the United States.

Visitors (Non-Residents) — Declare the value of all articles that will remain in the United States.

Declare all articles on this declaration form and show the value in U.S. dollars. For gifts, please indicate the retail value.

Duty — CBP officers will determine duty. U.S. residents are normally entitled to a duty-free exemption of $800 on items accompanying them. Visitors (non-residents) are normally entitled to an exemption of $100. Duty will be assessed at the current rate on the first $1,000 above the exemption.

Agricultural and Wildlife Products — To prevent the entry of dangerous agricultural pests and prohibited wildlife, the following are restricted: Fruits, vegetables, plants, plant products, soil, meat, meat products, birds, snails, and other live animals or animal products. Failure to declare such items to a Customs and Border Protection Officer/Customs and Border Protection Agriculture Specialist/Fish and Wildlife Inspector can result in penalties and the items may be subject to seizure.

Controlled substances, obscene articles, and toxic substances are generally prohibited entry.

Thank You, and Welcome to the United States.

The transportation of currency or **monetary instruments,** regardless of the amount, is legal. However, if you bring in to or take out of the United States more than $10,000 (U.S. or foreign equivalent, or a combination of both), you are required by law to file a report on FinCEN 105 (formerly Customs Form 4790) with U.S. Customs and Border Protection. Monetary instruments include coin, currency, travelers checks and bearer instruments such as personal or cashiers checks and stocks and bonds. If you have someone else carry the currency or monetary instrument for you, you must also file a report on FinCEN 105. Failure to file the required report or failure to report the *total* amount that you are carrying may lead to the seizure of *all* the currency or monetary instruments, and may subject you to civil penalties and/or criminal prosecution. SIGN ON THE OPPOSITE SIDE OF THIS FORM AFTER YOU HAVE READ THE IMPORTANT INFORMATION ABOVE AND MADE A TRUTHFUL DECLARATION.

Description of Articles (List may continue on another CBP Form 6059B)	Value	CBP Use Only
Total		

PAPERWORK REDUCTION ACT NOTICE: The Paperwork Reduction Act says we must tell you why we are collecting this information, how we will use it, and whether you have to give it to us. The information collected on this form is needed to carry out the Customs, Agriculture, and currency laws of the United States. CBP requires the information on this form to insure that travelers are complying with these laws and to allow us to figure and collect the right amount of duty and tax. Your response is mandatory. An agency may not conduct or sponsor, and a person is not required to respond to a collection of information, unless it displays a valid OMB control number. The estimated average burden associated with this collection of information is 4 minutes per respondent or record keeper depending on individual circumstances. Comments concerning the accuracy of this burden estimate and suggestions for reducing this burden should be directed to U.S. Customs and Border Protection, Reports Clearance Officer, Information Services Branch, Washington, DC 20229, and to the Office of Management and Budget, Paperwork Reduction Project (1651-0009), Washington, DC 20503. **THIS FORM MAY NOT BE REPRODUCED WITHOUT APPROVAL FROM THE CBP FORMS MANAGER.**

GPO: U.S. GOVERNMENT PRINTING OFFICE: 2008—570-089/80027 CBP Form 6059B (10/07)

■ Visas (사증)

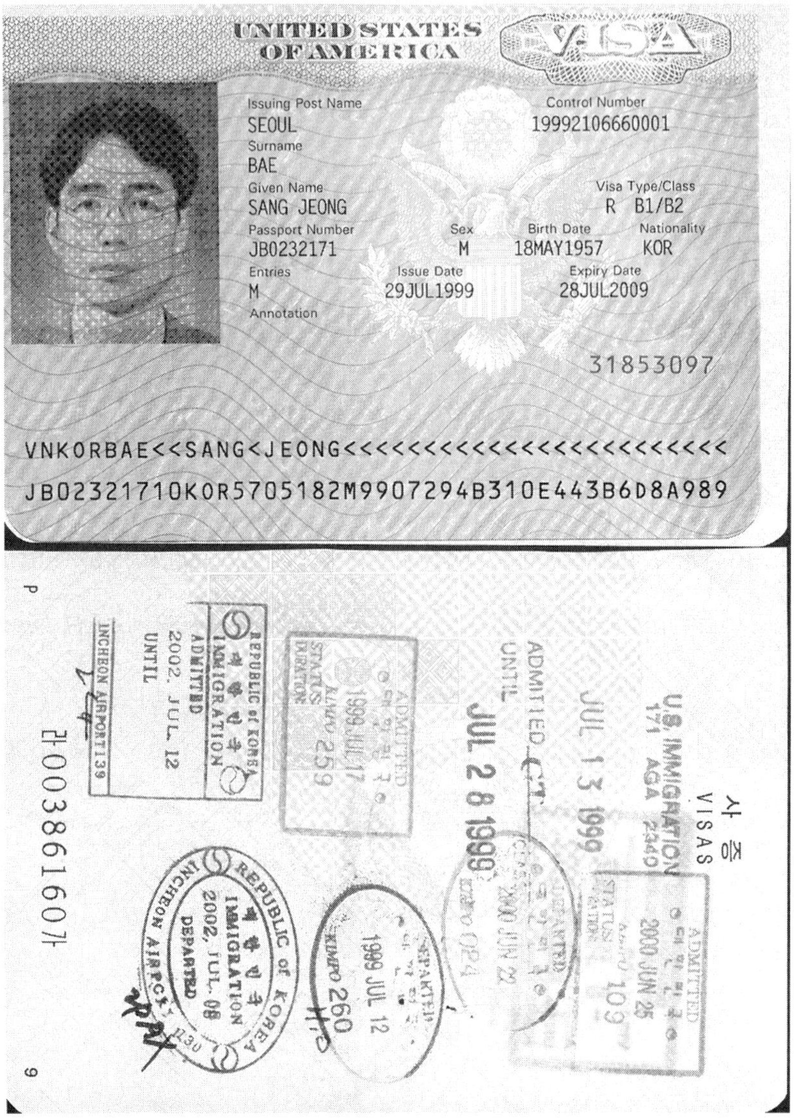

■ Quarantine & Security Information

QUARANTINE & SECURITY INFORMATION 검역 및 보안 안내

모든 입국 여행자는 건강에 이상이 있거나 농·축·수산물을 휴대한 경우 반드시 사전 신고하여 검역을 받으셔야 합니다.
Travelers who have disease-like symptoms, or are bringing in plants, meat or fish, must go through the quarantine process.

입국시 검역질문서 작성 검역전염병 오염지역인 동남아시아, 중남미에서 입국하는 모든 여행자는 검역질문서를 제출해야 하며, 발열, 설사, 구토 등의 증상이 있을 경우 신고해야 합니다. 이를 기피할 경우 최고 500만원의 벌금이 부과됩니다.

세균 · 바이러스 검사 서비스 안내 전염병 의심 여행객을 대상으로 콜레라, 장티푸스 등 세균 · 바이러스 검사를 무료로 실시합니다. 문의 032-740-2700

황열예방접종 안내 아프리카 및 중남미의 적도인근 국가로 여행하기 10일 전에 의무적으로 황열 예방접종을 해야 하며, 국제공인예방접종증명서 (Yellow Card)를 요구하는 국가도 있습니다.
관련문의: 국립인천공항검역소 http://nqs.cdc.go.kr/incheon-airport / 해외여행질병정보센터 http://travelinfo.cdc.go.kr

농산물 모든 식물류는 병원균(病原菌)이나 해충(害蟲) 감염 검사를 하며, 과실류와 흙이 묻어 있는 식물은 반입할 수 없습니다. 문의 1588-5117

축산물 육류와 육가공품은 당해 국가의 동물 검역 기관에서 발행한 증명서를 휴대해야 반입이 가능합니다. 신고를 하지 않아 적발되면 500만 원의 과태료가 부과(미국의 경우 $50~$250)됩니다. 조류인플루엔자와 구제역을 예방하기 위해서는 여행시 농장 방문을 자제하고, 개인 위생을 철저히 해야 합니다. 문의 1588-9060

수산물 살아있는 수산동물을 휴대하여 반입하고자 하면 수출국 정부기관이 발행하는 검역증명서(자가소비용 검역을 제외)를 제출해야 합니다. 위반시 300만 원 이하의 과태료를 부과하고 있습니다.
※ 자가소비용 범위 : 총중량 5kg 이내, 해외 총 취득가격 10만원 이내

Declare it, Dump it, Or pay a fine!

국립검역소 http://nqs.cdc.go.kr
국립식물검역원 www.npqs.go.kr
국립수의과학검역원 www.nvrqs.go.kr
국립수산물품질검사원 www.nfis.go.kr

항공기 내 액체류 휴대 반입 제한 안내 국제민간항공기구(ICAO)의 권고에 따라 액체폭탄 테러 위협에 대비하고자 미국, 캐나다, EU에서 이미 시행 중이며 한국, 일본, 대만, 호주 등이 액체류 휴대 반입을 제한하게 됩니다. 100㎖ 이하의 액체류 용기들을 투명하고 봉인 가능한 1ℓ 이하의 비닐 봉투 안에 담았을 경우, 기내 휴대 반입이 가능합니다.

Health Questionnaire If you are arriving from Southeast Asia, or Central or South America, you must submit a health questionnaire. Also, if you are suffering from such symptoms as fever or diarrhea, you must inform the quarantine officer. Failure to observe these regulations could result in a fine of up to 5 million won.

Virus Testing Service Any travelers who think they might have contracted bacterial or viral diseases such as typhoid or cholera can be tested free of charge. For more information, call 032-740-2700.

Yellow Fever Vaccination Any travelers going to Equatorial countries in Africa, or Central or South America must be inoculated against yellow fever at least 10 days before departure. For more information, visit the Incheon Airport National Quarantine Station website: http://nqs.cdc.go.kr/incheon-airport

Plants and Crops Inspectors will examine all plants and crops to determine if they are free of pests and diseases. The import of most tropical fruits and plants with soil is prohibited whether or not the commodities are pest-free. For information, call 1588-5117.

Meats and Meat Products Meats and meat products must come with a certificate issued by the animal quarantine authorities at the country of origin. If you are found carrying such items without having declared them, you could be fined up to 5 million won.

Fish and Crustacea Anyone bringing live marine animals into Korea must submit a quarantine certificate issued by the authorities at the country of origin. If you are found carrying such items without having declared them, you could be fined up to 3 million won.

Restrictions on Carrying Liquids Aboard Aircraft In order to prevent the use of liquids and aerosols in explosive devices, all such items should be carried in containers with a capacity no greater than 100ml. The containers should be placed in a transparent re-sealable plastic bag no larger than 1 liter in capacity. Passengers may carry only one plastic bag. As oversized plastic bags may be confiscated by security personnel, it is advised that excess amounts be checked in with your luggage. If you have any questions, please ask our staff or visit our website: www.koreanair.com.

■ Customs procedures

CUSTOMS PROCEDURES 휴대품 통관 안내

모든 입국 여행자는 여행자 휴대품 신고서를 작성하여 세관 직원에게 제출해야 합니다.

All passengers arriving from foreign countries must submit a customs declaration form.

韓国に入国するすべての旅行者は旅行者携帯品申告書を作成し、税関職員に提出する必要があります。

所有入境旅行者必须填写手提物品申报书并交写税关负责人。

휴대품 신고 대상 물품 면세 범위 초과 물품, 위조·모조·변조 화폐, 식품류, 마약류 및 비아그라, 무기류, 화약류, 유독성 또는 방사능 물질, 야생 동·식물 및 이들을 사용해 만든 제품, 판매 목적 물품, 회사용품, US$10,000을 초과하는 외화 또는 원화.

여행자 휴대품 면세 범위 여행자 휴대품 면세 범위는 US$400입니다.

* 다음 물품은 위 면세 범위와 별도로 면세됩니다. 주류 1병 1리터 이하, US$400 이하, 담배 한 보루 200개비, 향수 60밀리리터 단, 미성년자(만 19세 미만)에게는 주류, 담배 면세가 제외됩니다.

농림축수산물 및 한약재 면세 범위 * 1인당 총량 50kg 이내, 해외 취득 가격이 10만 원 이내이고, 검역에 합격해야 합니다. 참기름, 참깨, 꿀, 고사리, 더덕 5kg / 잣 1kg / 쇠고기 10kg / 기타 농산물은 품목당 5kg 이내 / 인삼, 상황버섯 300g / 녹용 150g / 기타 한약재는 품목당 3kg 이내

면세 범위 초과 물품에 대한 통관 여행중 구입 물품 중 US$1,000 (US$400 제외) 이하까지는 단일간이세율 20%가 적용됩니다. 녹용·향수·담배·주류·농림축산물 등은 기본 세율이 적용됩니다. 상업용 물품은 수입신고를 해야 합니다.

세금 사후 납부 제도 자진 신고한 여행자의 과세 물품은 물건을 먼저 찾아가고 세금은 금융기관에 사후 납부(15일 이내)할 수 있습니다.

출국 시 세관 신고 입국 시 다시 반입할 고가의 물품 등은 출국 시, 여러 번 반·출입하는 물품은 최초 1회만 신고하면 됩니다. US$10,000 이상 외화 및 원화를 휴대 반출 시에도 신고해야 합니다.

* 문화재 및 이에 준하는 물품은 반출이 제한됩니다.

면세 물품 구입 시 유의사항 출국 시 면세 물품 구매 한도는 1인당 US$3,000지만, 입국 시 면세 범위는 US$400이며, 초과분은 세관 신고 후 세금을 납부해야 합니다. **관련사항 문의** 관세청 www.customs.go.kr 인천공항세관 www.customs.go.kr/airport 관세종합상담센터 1577-8577 인천공항세관 민원상담 032-722-4414 * 입국 시 궁금한 사항이 있거나 세관 안내가 필요한 경우에는 1층 입국장에서 안내도우미 Green Cap을 찾으세요.

해외여행 시 마약 운반에 연루되지 않도록 주의하세요 마약 운반을 수락하거나 직접 복용하다 현지 당국에 적발되면, 5~7년이라는 장기간의 수형 생활을해야 하며, 국가 이미지 손상은 물론 우리 국민들이 해외 공항·항만을 통과할 때 까다로운 심사를 받는 결과를 초래할 수 있으니 피해를 입지 않기 위해 특히 주의해야 합니다. * 국가정보원 국제범죄정보센터 Tel : 111 홈페이지 www.nis.go.kr

Goods to Declare Goods exceeding the duty-free allowance; forged bills; wild plants or any products made from them; meats; agricultural/ forestry/ fishery products and any other foodstuffs; illicit drugs; weapons, bullets, explosives or toxic substances; commercial goods for sale; Korean or foreign currencies worth over US$10,000.

Duty-free Goods for personal use with a total value of not more than US$400. One bottle (less than 1 liter) of hard liquor, 200 cigarettes and 60 milliliters of perfume. (Minors aged 19 or under have no duty-free allowance for alcohol or cigarettes.)

Duty-free Allowance on Agricultural / Forestry / Fishery Products *The total value of such products cannot exceed 100,000 won, their total weight cannot exceed 50kg, and they must be quarantined at customs. Further restrictions: sesame oil, sesame, honey 5kg / beef 10kg/ ginseng 300g / deer antlers 150g / other medical herbs 3kg each

Customs Clearance on Excess Goods If the total value of goods exceeding the US$400 duty-free allowance is under US$1,000, a 20% flat rate tariff will be applied. Different rates will be applied for agricultural products, cigarettes, liquor, etc. However, all goods being brought in for commercial purposes must be declared.

Clearing Customs after Date of Arrival For passengers who declare excess goods, items exceeding the duty-free allowance can be claimed first, and any duties can be paid at a bank or post office within 15 days of the issuance of a payment order.

Customs Declaration If you have packed valuable items that you plan to bring back, you can declare them when leaving Korea. Korean and foreign currencies worth US$10,000 or more must be declared. It is illegal to take items deemed "cultural assets" out of Korea.

Tips on Buying Duty-free The duty-free allowance for travelers leaving Korea is US$3,000; on return, it is US$400. Duty must be paid on any items whose collective value exceeds those amounts. **Information:** Korea Customs Service: www.customs.go.kr

Narcotics Any travelers caught with illicit drugs will face a prison sentence of between 5 and 7 years. For more information or to report any illicit drug-related activity, dial 111 for the National Intelligence Service International Crime Information Center.

2 Patterns Drill

(1) Have a nice trip.

good time

great

wonderful

(2) How long are you going to stay in U.S.A?

Canada

Seoul

Singapore

this country

I am going to stay for 5 days

(3) What' s the purpose of your visit?

I' m here for sightseeing.

travel

visiting my relatives

on business

3 Utterance-Response Drills

Did I fill this form out correctly?

Yes, it seems all right.

What's the purpose of your trip?

For sightseeing./ On business.

What's your reason for entering the U.S.?

To visit an old friend.

How long are you going to stay?

I'm going to stay for 3 days.

May I see your customs declaration?

Yes, here it is.

Do you have anything to declare?

Just a few gifts.

Are you a visitor or resident?

A visitor. I'm travelling on business.

Do you have anything to declare, sir?

No, I don't. / No, I have nothing declare.

What do you have in your baggage, sir?

They're all my personal effects.

OK. Everything is cleared. You can go, sir. Have a nice trip.

Thank you.

4 Dialogue

Dialogue A

O : Immigration Officer P : Passenger

O : May I see your passport? 여권 좀 보여주시겠습니까?

P : Here it is. 여기 있습니다.

O : What's the purpose of your visit? 방문 목적이 무엇입니까?

P : (I'm here) for sightseeing. 관광차 왔습니다.

O : How long are you going to stay in the States?
미국에 얼마동안 체류하실 예정입니까?

P : (I'm staying for) about six days. 약 6일 동안 체류할 예정입니다.

O : Where will you be staying? 어디에서 머무십니까?

P : (I will be staying) at the Hilton Hotel. 힐튼호텔에서 머물 것입니다.

외국공항에 도착해서 수화물을 찾은 후 이민국(출입국 관리소)을 통과하는데 이민국 직원들이 꼭 물어보는 질문이 방문목적이다. 대개의 경우 관광(sightseeing)이 주된 목적이지만 친척방문일 경우 For visiting my relatives. 사업상일 경우 On business. 라고 대답하면 된다.

이러한 질문과 대답은 대부분 입국 신고서에 기재되어 있기 때문에 입국신고서 기재난에 정확하게 기재되어 있으면 질문을 하지 않는 경우가 대부분이다.

유용한 표현들

I'm here to enjoy my vacation. 휴가를 즐기기 위해서 왔습니다.
I'm here for meeting my friend. 친구를 만나기 위해서 왔습니다.
I'm staying at my uncle's house. 저의 삼촌 집에서 머물 예정입니다.

Dialogue B

O : Customs Officer, P : Passenger

O : Do you have anything to declare? 신고할 물건이 있으십니까?

P : No, I have nothing (to declare). 아니오, 없습니다.

O : How about money? Do you have more than $5,000?
현금은요? 5,000달러 이상을 소지하고 있습니까?

P : No, I don't. 아니오, 없습니다.

O : Are you bringing in any agricultural products such as fruits or seeds?
과일이나 씨앗 같은 농산물을 가지고 들어오십니까?

P : No, I'm not. 아닙니다.

O : Do you have any liquor, cigarettes or gifts?
술, 담배 혹은 선물들을 소지하고 있습니까?

P : Yes, I have small gifts and one bottle of whiskey.
예, 저는 약간의 선물과 위스키 한 병을 소지하고 있습니다.

세관을 통과할 때 세관직원이 주로 물어보는 질문 내용이다. 세관 신고서(Customs Declaration Form)의 기재 난에 정확하게 기재되어 있으면 대개의 경우 그냥 통과하지만, 만약의 경우를 대비해서 질문에 대한 대답은 알아두어야 하겠다. 어느 나라든지 농산물, 술, 담배, 고가의 물건 등은 반입 한도를 초과했을 때에는 규제를 하고 있으니 여행 전에 반입 한도를 알아보는 지혜도 필요하다.

유용한 표현들

May I see your customs declaration form?
세관신고서를 보여 주시겠습니까?

Would you open your bag? 가방을 열어 주시겠습니까?

O.K. Everything is cleared. 좋습니다. 이상이 없군요.

You may go now. 자, 가셔도 됩니다.

Dialogue *C*

T : Tourist, P : Passenger, O : Officer

T : Excuse me. Could you show me the way to the Korean Embassy?
실례합니다만 한국대사관으로 가는 길을 알려 주시겠습니까?

P : Sure. It's right over there. You can see the Korean flag?
물론이지요. 바로 저곳에 있습니다. 태극기가 보이시지요?

T : Thank you.
고맙습니다.

O : May I help you?
무엇을 도와드릴까요?

T : Yes. I lost my passport. I'd like to have it reissued.
네. 여권을 분실했습니다. 재발급을 받고 싶습니다.

O : When and where did you lose it?
언제 어디에서 분실했습니까?

T : I think I lost it in the bus this afternoon.
오늘 오후에 버스 안에서 잃어버린 것 같습니다.

O : Please fill out this form.
이 양식을 작성해 주십시오.

여권을 분실하면 여행국의 한국대사관에서 임시여권을 발급 받아야 하는데 이때 사진이 필요하니 외국여행을 할 때는 만일의 경우를 대비해서 사진을 준비하고, 여권번호 등은 따로 수첩에 기록해 놓는 것이 좋다.

Dialogue D

T : Tourist, O : Officer

O : May I help you? 도와드릴까요?

T : Yes, I lost my suitcase. 네, 여행가방을 분실했습니다.

O : When and where did you lose it? 언제 어디에서 분실했습니까?

T : On the bus, that I took at about 7:00 P.M. yesterday from the international Airport.
어제 오후 7시경 국제공항에서 타고 왔던 버스에서 분실했습니다.

O : Can you describe the contents of your suitcase, please?
여행가방의 내용물이 무엇인지를 말씀해 주시겠습니까?

T : All my valuables and personal effects were in it..
모든 귀중품과 개인용품이 들어있습니다.

O : All right. Please fill out this form and sign here.
알겠습니다. 이 양식을 작성해주시고 서명해 주십시오.
We'll contact you as soon as we find it.
찾는 대로 바로 연락드리겠습니다.

여행 가방이나 소지품을 분실하게 되면 공항 Lost and Found(분실, 습득물 보관소)에 가서 신고를 하면 된다. 외국에서 소지품을 분실하게 되면 찾지 못하는 경우가 많으니 분실하지 않도록 사전에 주의하는 것이 좋다.

유용한 표현들

My bag is missing= My bag is gone. 제 가방이 없어졌습니다.

I had my passport, money and checks in my bag.
제 가방 속에는 여권, 돈, 그리고 수표가 들어있습니다.

5 Role Play

Student A

A : 다음 분, 안녕하세요?

B : Just fine.

A : 송 선생인가요?

B : That's correct.

A : 좋습니다. 미국에 와 보신 적이 있습니까?

B : Yes. I have.

A : 좋습니다. 이번 여행의 목적은 무엇입니까?

B : I'll be visiting some friends and taking some tours.

A : 좋습니다. 과일이나 고기, 식물, 채소 같은 것들을 갖고 들어오십니까?

B : No.

A : 식품이나 뭐 부패할 것들은 없나요?

B : No.

A : 현금은 얼마나 갖고 계시나요? 5,000불 이상입니까?

B : No.

A : 좋습니다. 선물이나 기념물을 갖고 계십니까?

B : Ah... Yes, I brought some.

A : 기념품은 모두 얼마쯤 됩니까?

B : About $250.

A : 250달러 정도라고요. 좋습니다. 가셔서 이것을 위층에 있는 세관에 제출하십시오. 오신 것을 환영합니다. 안녕히 가십시오.

Student *B*

A : Next, please. How are you?

B : 네, 안녕하세요.

A : OK. You are Mr. Song?

B : 맞습니다.

A : OK. Have you been in the United States before?

B : 예, 그렇습니다.

A : OK. What's the purpose of your travel today?

B : 친구들 좀 만나고, 관광도 하려고 합니다.

A : OK, and are you bringing in any fruits, meats, plants, or vegetables?

B : 아닙니다.

A : Anything edible or perishable?

B : 없습니다.

A : How about money? Do you have in excess of $5,000?

B : 아닙니다.

A : OK. You bring any gifts of souvenirs?

B : 아, 네. 갖고 있습니다.

A : What's the total value of the souvenirs?

B : 250달러 쯤 됩니다.

A : About $250, OK. Go ahead and present this upstairs to customs. Welcome over. Bye.

Unit 02 In Flight

1 Vocabulary and Patterns

* airline ticket(passenger ticket) 항공권

one-way ticket 편도 항공권 / round trip ticket 왕복 항공권

* first class 일등석/ economy class 일반석

* boarding pass 탑승권

EX

A : Excuse me. 20G is my seat number. Where is it?
B : Would you show me your boarding pass?
This way, please. Your seat is just over there.

* window seat 창 쪽 좌석 / aisle seat 통로 쪽 좌석

EX

A : Would you like a window seat or an aisle seat?
B : Window seat, please.

* rest room, toilet 화장실 / vacant 비어있음 / occupied 사용 중
* flight attendant(crew) 승무원
  steward 남자 승무원 / stewardess 여자 승무원
* cockpit 조종실, 조종석 / captain 기장
* call button 승무원 호출버튼 / channel switch 채널선택 스위치
  reading light 독서등

* seat belt, safety belt 안전벨트(항공사 승무원 영어문제)

EX

A : Please fasten your seatbelt.
B : Would you show me how to fasten this seatbelt?
A : I'm sorry this seatbelt doesn't work.

* overhead compartment(rack) 좌석 위의 문 달린 선반

EX

A : Where shall I put my briefcase?
B : You can put your briefcase under your seat or on the rack over your seat.

* forced landing 비상착륙 / emergency exit 비상구
* life jacket(vest) 구명조끼 / oxygen mask 산소 마스크

* airsickness 비행기 멀미/ carsickness 차멀미 / seasickness 뱃멀미
  airsick bag 위생봉지
* motion sickness pill 멀미약(TEPS Voca. Part I)

EX

A : Can you wait for me here? Before our flight, I need to find a pharmacy to buy some _____ sickness pills.
B : Really? I didn't know you have airsickness.
(a) movement (b) mobility (c) locomotion (d) motion

★d

* toilet paper 화장지 / waste bin 쓰레기통
* Welcome aboard : 선장, 기장, 승무원들이 승객에게 탑승 시 하게 되는 환영인사.

* have a reservation 예약하다 / 자리를 예약하다 book one's reservations / in person 스스로, 본인이

EX

To schedule the early flight, passengers must book their _______ in person. (TOEIC R/C Part V)
(A) advance (B) resolution (C) restoration (D) reservations

★d

Put the following into English. 항공사 승무원 영어문제

신사 숙녀 여러분 안녕하십니까? 노스웨스트 항공에 탑승하신 것을 환영합니다. 저희 767 항공기는 L.A를 향해 출발하려고 합니다. 좌석을 바로해 주시고, 안전벨트를 착용하시고, 기내에서 이동전화나, FM 라디오, CD 플레이어 등의 사용을 자제해 주시기 바랍니다. 감사합니다.

Good morning, ladies and gentlemen.

We welcome you aboard North West Airlines. This flight 767 is now leaving for LAX.

Please, put your seat in the upright position, fasten your seatbelt, and refrain from using cellular phone, FM radios and CD player in the cabin. Thank you.

+ 「~해야 합니까?」

Do I have / need to + 동사원형~?

Is it necessary to + 동사원형~?

EX

Do I have to take any tests?
Do I need to send a photograph?

■ Boarding Pass(탑승권)

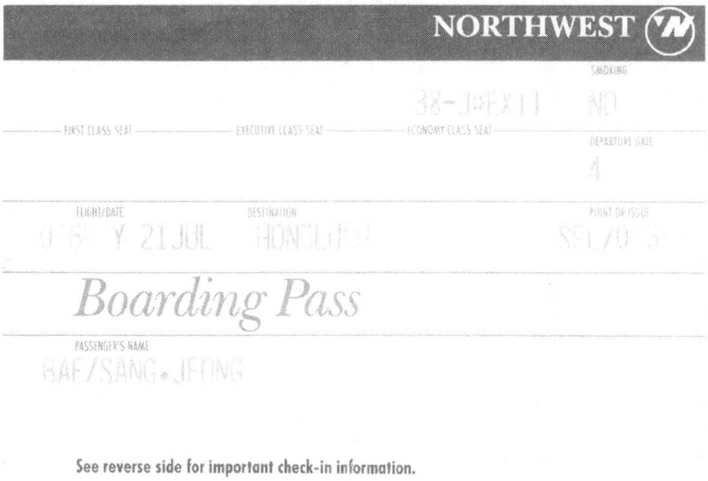
NORTHWEST

SMOKING NO

FIRST CLASS SEAT | EXECUTIVE CLASS SEAT | ECONOMY CLASS SEAT 38-J*EXIT

DEPARTURE GATE 4

FLIGHT/DATE | DESTINATION | POINT OF ISSUE

Boarding Pass

PASSENGER'S NAME BAE/SANG•JEONG

See reverse side for important check-in information.

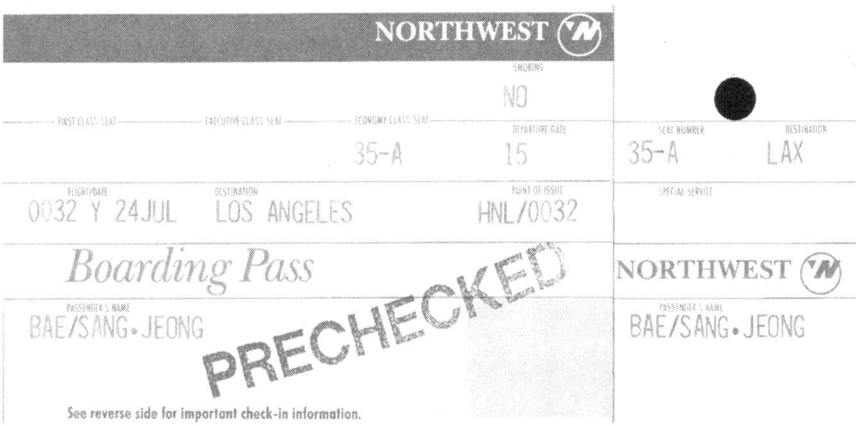
NORTHWEST

SMOKING NO

FIRST CLASS SEAT | EXECUTIVE CLASS SEAT | ECONOMY CLASS SEAT 35-A | DEPARTURE GATE 15

FLIGHT/DATE 0032 Y 24JUL | DESTINATION LOS ANGELES | POINT OF ISSUE HNL/0032

Boarding Pass

PRECHECKED

PASSENGER'S NAME BAE/SANG•JEONG

See reverse side for important check-in information.

SEAT NUMBER 35-A | DESTINATION LAX

SPECIAL SERVICE

NORTHWEST

PASSENGER'S NAME BAE/SANG•JEONG

SINGAPORE AIRLINES

Economy Class Boarding Pass

FLIGHT SQ 0882 DESTN. SEL CLASS Y BOARDING TIME 2250

DATE 15JUL SEAT 40H GATE F077

NAME BAE SANGJEONGMR

REMARKS Please proceed for boarding

PLEASE BE PRESENT AT THE BOARDING GATE 30 MINUTES BEFORE DEPARTURE TIME

Economy Class

THAI AIRWAYS INTL.

BAE.SANGJEONGMR
TAIPEI TG0634 Y 23OCT
SEOUL

BOARDING PASS

Seat 68A YES

Seq No. 78 0/ 0

Thai

USAir Passenger Ticket and Baggage Check RECEIPT

3B221ODP 2149865208 1016 SFO-ATO US 29JUL91

BAE/S

VOID VOID VOID VOID VOID

NONREF/CHANGE/NO REFUND

FP CA KMK-TDCK ONE BAG /FC 29JUL SFOUSLAX 53.64H9NR $53.64 END

FARE USD 53.64
TAX US 5.36
TOTAL USD 59.00

0041201723 3 0 037 2149865208 2

DO NOT MARK OR WRITE IN THE WHITE AREA ABOVE

Emirates

NAME OF PASSENGER BAE/SANGJEONGMR

FROM SEOUL ICN

TO DUBAI

FLIGHT CLASS DATE TIME
323 Y 13AUG 0030

GATE BOARDING TIME SEAT SMOKE
32 2345 34E NO

PCS WT UNCKD BAGGAGE ID NUMBER
0007

DOCUMENT NUMBER CPN

Emirates

NAME OF PASSENGER BAE/SANGJEONGMR

FROM DUBAI

TO ROME FCO

FLIGHT CLASS DATE TIME
EK 097 Y 13AUG 0755

GATE BOARDING TIME SEAT SMOKE
0710 40B NO

PCS WT UNCKD BAGGAGE ID NUMBER
0003

DOCUMENT NUMBER CPN

■ Passenger Ticket(항공권)

e-Ticket Itinerary/Receipt

Print 1834/27MAR

송객성명 Passenger Name BAE/SANGJEONGMR

e-티켓번호 e-Ticket number 0145727300022-023

POWERED BY TOPAS

· 여정 Itinerary

예약번호 Booking Reference 139-1636

출발 도착 Departure Arrival	Class 클래스	Date 날짜	Time 시간	Terminal 터미널	Status 예약상태	Not Valid 유효기간		Baggage Allowance 무료수하물 허용량	Reference 예약번호
						Before 시작	After 종료		
SEOUL ICN VANCOLVER YVR	L	04MAY08 04MAY08	1710 1125	M	OK		04JUN	2PC	LLMS6E
	AC 64 OPERATED BY AIR CANADA								FareBasis 운임 L3MOKC/CG00
VANCOUVER YVR SAN FRANCISCO SFO	L	09MAY08 09MAY08	1110 1332	M 3	OK		04JUN	2PC	LLMS6E
	AC 566 OPERATED BY AIR CANADA								FareBasis 운임 L3MOKC/CG00
LOS ANGELES LAX VANCOUVER YVR	L	14MAY08 14MAY08	0700 0945	2 M	OK		04JUN	2PC	LLMS6E
	AC 551 OPERATED BY AIR CANADA								FareBasis 운임 L3MOKC/CG00
VANCOUVER YVR SEOUL ICN	L	14MAY08 15MAY08	1215 1540	M	OK		04JUN	2PC	LLMS6E
	AC 63 OPERATED BY AIR CANADA								FareBasis 운임 L3MOKC/CG00

· 항공사 직원을 위한 e-티켓 정보입니다. For Airline Staff

Restriction	NON-ENDS/CIC*50/KR08R S8GV0051F1
Coni.Ticket No.	
Fare Calculation	M*SEL AC YVR AC SFO M0.00/-LAX AC X/YVR AC SEL M0.00 NUC0.00END ROE922.32 XT 173200YQ 28000BP 16700CA 800XG 14700SQ 5600YC 15600US 15600US 5100XA 7100XY 2600AY 4600XF LAX4.5
Tour Code	KR08R
Fare Amount	KRW0
Equiv. Fare Paid	
TAX	KRW 289600XT
Total Amount	KRW289600
Form of Payment	: CASH
e-Ticket Issue Date/Place	27MAR08 / (주)하나투어 /17305304 / 하나투어 / 02-2127-1216

■ Asiana Fleet

B737-400

cruising speed (km/h)	경제운항속도	790
max. flight distance (km)	최대운항거리	1,463
max. cruising hour (hr:mn)	최대운항시간	2:00
max. altitude (m)	최대운항고도	11,278
length (m)	길이	36.45
height (m)	높이	11.13
wing span (m)	날개폭	28.88

B767-300S, B767-300F

cruising speed (km/h)	경제운항속도	853
max. flight distance (km)	최대운항거리	6,695/7,538/5,926
max. cruising hour (hr:mn)	최대운항시간	8:04/9:02/7:00
max. altitude (m)	최대운항고도	13,137
length (m)	길이	54.94
height (m)	높이	15.85
wing span (m)	날개폭	47.57

B747-400, B747-400 COMBI, B747-400F, B747-400SF

cruising speed (km/h)	경제운항속도	907
max. flight distance (km)	최대운항거리	12,890/13,297/7,519/7,408
max. cruising hour (hr:mn)	최대운항시간	14:14/14:44/8:20/8:15
max. altitude (m)	최대운항고도	13,746
length (m)	길이	70.66
height (m)	높이	19.41
wing span (m)	날개폭	64.44

B777-200ER

cruising speed (km/h)	경제운항속도	894
max. flight distance (km)	최대운항거리	11,603
max. cruising hour (hr:mn)	최대운항시간	13:07
max. altitude (m)	최대운항고도	13,137
length (m)	길이	62.70
height (m)	높이	18.40
wing span (m)	날개폭	60.90

A320-232

cruising speed (km/h)	경제운항속도	841
max. flight distance (km)	최대운항거리	4,000/4,611
max. cruising hour (hr:mn)	최대운항시간	5:01/5:45
max. altitude (m)	최대운항고도	12,131
length (m)	길이	37.57
height (m)	높이	11.76
wing span (m)	날개폭	34.09

A321-131, A321-231

cruising speed (km/h)	경제운항속도	841
max. flight distance (km)	최대운항거리	2,092/4,232/4,592/4,797
max. cruising hour (hr:mn)	최대운항시간	2:37/5:14/5:41/5:56
max. altitude (m)	최대운항고도	11,918/12,131
length (m)	길이	44.51
height (m)	높이	11.76
wing span (m)	날개폭	34.10

A330-323

cruising speed (km/h)	경제운항속도	876
max. flight distance (km)	최대운항거리	9,316
max. cruising hour (hr:mn)	최대운항시간	11:09
max. altitude (m)	최대운항고도	12,527
length (m)	길이	63.70
height (m)	높이	16.84
wing span (m)	날개폭	60.30

2 Patterns Drill

(1) May I see your boarding pass?
passenger ticket
embarkation card
I.D card

(2) What kinds of beverage do you have?
soft drink
wine
whiskey

(3) May I have a blanket?
pillow
newspaper
magazine

(4) Would you like something to drink?
read
want
need

3 Utterance-Response Drills

Welcome aboard KAL.

Thank you.

Can you tell me where my seat is?

Yes. This is a window seat, sir.

May I see your boarding pass, please?

Yes. here it is.

Good morning, ma'am. Would you like a glass of wine?

Can I have a glass of orange juice instead of wine?

Certainly, ma'am.

Would you like a newspaper, sir?

Do you have the Wall-Street Journal?

I'm sorry but we don't have it on board.

How about the New York Times?

That'll be nice.

What is the time in New York?

The local time is three in the afternoon, sir?

Miss, where are the rest rooms?

Right in the back of this aisle.

Sir, we are taking orders for dinner. Would you like chicken of beef?

I'd like the beef, please.

Could I have something to drink, Miss?

Sure.

Do you have juice?

Yes. Orange, pineapple, and tomato, sir.

I'll have a tomato, please.

Please fill out this customs declaration.

All right. Thank you.

Can you help me with this declaration form?

I'll be right with you, ma'am.

Do I need to give you this form?

No, ma'am. Hand it to the officer.

4 Dialogue

Dialogue A

S : Stewardess, P : Passenger

S : Would you like something to drink? 마실 것 좀 드릴까요?

P : Yes, what kinds of beverage do you have?
예, 어떤 종류의 음료수가 있습니까?

S : We have coffee, tea, orange juice, coke, beer etc.
커피, 홍차, 오렌지 주스, 콜라, 맥주 등이 있습니다.

P : I'd like coffee, please. 커피 주세요.

S : Cream or sugar? 크림이나 설탕은요?

P : Both, please. 둘 다 주세요.

S : Here you go. 여기 있습니다.

P : Thank you. 고맙습니다.

외국 항공기를 이용할 경우 기내에서 음료 서비스를 받을 때 영어가 사용된다. 이런 상황에서 한국인들이 흔히 실수하는 부분은 cream을 달라고 해야 하는데 Frima(프리마), please라고 말하는 경우가 많다. 프리마는 동서식품에서 제조한 커피 크림의 상표명으로 외국인들은 무엇을 의미하는지 알지 못한다. 콜라를 주문할 때도 Cola, Please 하는 경우가 많은데 이럴 때는 Coke, please라고 말해야 콜라를 서비스 받을 수 있다.

유용한 표현들

What kinds of wine(포도주) do you have?
We have red wine and white wine.
What kinds of juice(주스) do you have ?
Orange juice, tomato juice, grape juice and pineapple juice.

Dialogue *B*

S : What would you like, sir? 손님. 무엇을 드시겠습니까?

P : What kinds of food do you have? 어떤 종류가 있습니까?

S : We have beef and fish. 쇠고기, 생선이 있습니다.

P : (I'd like) fish, please. 생선으로 주세요.

S : We are sorry, we don't have fish. 죄송합니다만 생선이 떨어졌습니다.

P : Then beef, please. 그러면 쇠고기로 주세요.

S : Here you go. 여기 있습니다.

P : Thank you. 고맙습니다.

기내에서 기내식을 제공받는데, 외국 항공기를 이용할 경우 영어가 사용된다. 이런 상황에서 영어가 서투른 승객들은 다른 승객이 먹는 음식을 손으로 가리키는 경우가 많다. 승무원이 Beef or fish? 혹은 Beef or chicken?이라고 말하면 그 중에 선호하는 음식을 하나 선택해서 쇠고기의 경우 Beef, please.라고 말하면 기내식을 서비스 받을 수 있다.

중국 항공기의 경우 Pork or fish?라고 말하는 경우도 있는데 이럴 땐 돼지고기와 생선 중에 좋아하는 것을 선택해서 주문하면 된다.

유용한 표현들

S : May I take your meal tray, sir? 식판을 가져가도 되겠습니까?

P : No, I'm not finished, yet. 아니오, 아직 식사를 다 못했습니다.

S : I'm sorry, sir. 죄송합니다, 손님

5 Role Play

Student A

A : 이번이 처음 항공 여행입니까?

B : No. This is my third.

A : 미국 어디로 가십니까?

B : To New York on business.

A : 저는 뉴욕에서 달라스 행으로 갈아 탈 겁니다.

B : I've been to Dallas. It's quite a large city.

A : 이 서식은 무엇입니까?

B : It's an I-94 form which must be filled in if you're an alien entering the U.S.A.

A : 이걸 어떻게 하는 거죠?

B : Give it to the Immigration Officer.
He will staple it to your passport.

A : 출입국 관리소는 어디에 있습니까?

B : As soon as you deplane, you will be led to the immigration section.

A : Would you like something to drink?

B : 예. 어떤 종류의 음료수가 있습니까?

A : We have coffee, tea, orange juice etc.

B : 커피로 먹겠습니다.

Student B

A : Is this your first flight?

B : 아뇨. 세 번째에요.

A : Where are you going in the U.S.A?

B : 사업차 뉴욕에 가는 길입니다.

A : I'll be making a connection in New York for Dallas.

B : 저도 달라스에 가 봤어요. 아주 큰 도시더군요.

A : What is this form?

B : 미국에 입국하는 외국인이면 작성해야 하는 I-94 서식입니다.

A : What do I do with it?

B : 이민국 직원에게 주세요. 그가 손님의 여권에 첨부해 드릴 겁니다.

A : Where is Immigration?

B : 비행기에서 내리시는 대로 이민국 구역으로 안내될 것입니다.

A : 음료수를 드시겠습니까?

B : Yes. What kind of beverage do you have?

A : 커피, 홍차, 오렌지주스 등이 있습니다.

B : I'd like coffee, please.

Unit 03

Getting Information

1 Vocabulary and Patterns

* sightseeing guidebook 관광안내책자

EX

A : Is there a sightseeing guidebook for this area?
B : Yes, here it is.

* timetable 시간표

EX

A : May I have a bus timetable, please?
B : Yes, here it is.

* commercial transportation 대중교통수단
* ground transportation 지상교통수단
* taxi stand 택시 정류장 / bus stop[버스탑]버스 정류장
  subway station = station, stop 지하철 역 / train station 기차역

EX

A : Where is the nearest bus stop?
B : Turn right at the next corner.

* change subway lines 지하철을 갈아타다.(TOEFL W/E)

EX

A : Where can I change subway lines?
B : You can change subway lines in Jongrosamga(stop).

* a Suseo-bound No.3 Line 수서 방향 3호선

EX

A : Would you show me the way to Gyengbuk Palace.
B : Take No.2 line to Uljirosamga and change to a Daewha-bound No.3 Line.

* get to (arrive at) ~에 닿다. ~에 이르다.

EX

How was you commute from Ilsan to Seoul? (TOEIC L/C part II)
(a) I get to Seoul by subway.
(b) It was bad.
(c) I like Ilsan better than Seoul.
(d) There are many people commuting from Ilsan to Seoul.

* have a good sense of direction 방향 감각이 좋다.

EX

W : What do you do when you're lost in downtown Seoul?
M : Oh, I never get lost.
W : Really? How's that?
M : ______________. (TEPS L/C)
(a) I always have a direction.
(b) I never know where I am.
(c) I have a good sense of direction.
(d) I wish I had a map.

유용한 표현들

안내소에서 ...

① Where can I catch a taxi?
어디서 택시를 탈 수 있습니까?

② How long does it take to go downtown?
시내까지 시간이 얼마나 걸립니까?

③ I'm looking for a hotel that costs about $40 per night.
하룻밤에 40달러 정도로 묵을 수 있는 호텔을 찾습니다.

④ Can I have a bus timetable, please?
버스 시간표 좀 얻을 수 있을까요?

⑤ Please tell us about the places of interest in this area.
이 지역의 명소를 알려 주십시오.

⑥ Where can I get a ticket for the limousine?
리무진 승차권을 어디서 살 수 있습니까?

⑦ Is there a sightseeing guidebook for this area?
이 지역의 관광지 안내 책자는 없습니까?

⑧ Where can I rent a car?
차를 빌리는 곳이 어디죠?

⑨ Can you help me? I left something on the plane.
좀 도와주시겠어요? 비행기에 뭘 놓고 내렸어요.

⑩ I can't find my sister. Could you page her?
제 누이를 못 찾겠습니다. 좀 불러 주시겠어요?

2 Patterns Drill

(1) Where should I get a taxi?
cab
bus
train
subway

(2) Please tell me what kind of trains there are?
buses
express bus
taxi

(3) What is the best way to go there?
most convenient
common
= How could I get there best?

(4) The bus leaves for Daejeon every ten minutes.
Seoul twenty
Busan half an hour
Gwangju

(5) May I buy a ticket in advance?
beforehand
ahead of time
before in time
early

3 Utterance-Response Drills

Traffic Information 교통안내

(1) Taxi

Excuse me, officer. Where should I get a taxi?

You may get a taxi at the taxi stand.

How much is the taxi fare?

The basic fare is 1,300 Won.

How about going out of the boundary of the city?

Yes, a 20% surcharge should be paid for driving out of the boundary of Jeonju city.

(2) Bus

Excuse me, sir. I'd like to go to Jeonju railway station. Which bus should I take?

You may take the bus number 14 or 104.

Can you tell me how to take the bus?

There are two kind of buses; a seat bus and an ordinary bus. The seat bus fare is 700Won and the ordinary bus is paid by a bus token or 380Won.

(3) Express Bus

What locations can you reach by the express bus?

You may go to any major city in the country. Where do you want to go?

I wish to go to Daejeon. How long does it take to go to Daejeon?

It will take about one hour and ten minutes.

Where can I get a ticket?

Please go to the ticket sales window number one.

(4) Railway Train

Please tell me what kind of trains there are?

There are four kinds of trains; super-express, extra-express, express and local trains.

How much does it cost by the super express train and how long does it take to Seoul?

The fare is 45,000 Won and it'll take about 3hours and 30 minutes.

(5) Airplane

I'd like to travel by airplanes. Where may I go in this country?

You may reach Seoul, Busan, Jeju island, etc.

Where can I buy an airplane ticket?

You may purchase an airplane ticket at any travel agency in downtown or hotel.

Excuse me, but where can I take a bus to the city?

I' m afraid, I don' t know, either. You can ask at the tourist information desk over there.

I need information on local hotels, please.
Yes, sir. What can I do for you?
We arrived without reservations and need a hotel in the downtown area.
Any particular hotel in mind, sir?
I' m not too familiar with hotel names. Could you suggest one, please?

Excuse me. Could you help me find a hotel for the night?
I' ll do what I can. What price range, sir?
A medium-priced hotel with a single room.
The Mayfair is a nice old hotel, sir.
I' ll take your word for it. Would you mind calling for me?
I' ll be glad to check for you.

Would you prefer one near this center?
About 10minutes walk from here would be fine. And it would be great if it' s fairly cheap.

Does the Hyatt Hotel send a van to pick up passengers?
Yes, they do.

How about a motel near the airport?
Let me check the two nearest ones.
You are very helpful. Thank you.

4 Dialogue

Dialogue A

A : Excuse me, officer. Where should I get a cab?

B : You may take a taxi at the front of a hotel.

A : How much is the taxi fare?

B : The basic fare is 1,300Won.

Dialogue B

A : Excuse me. May I ask a question?

B : Yes. Go ahead.

A : I want to go to the 2002 World Cup stadium. Which bus should I take?

B : You may take bus number 31 for Banweol.

Dialogue C

A : Excuse me. Where is the express bus terminal?

B : The express bus terminal is located at Banpo dong in downtown.

A : How can I get there?

B : Which do you want to take a bus or a taxi?

Dialogue 𝒟

A : Excuse me. How can I get a ticket for Seoul?

B : Right over there. You can get it at sales window number three.

A : Is there any classification on seats?

B : Yes, there is the first class and ordinary class.

Dialogue ℰ

A : Can you tell me where Asiana Air Line is?

B : Asiana Air Line? Yes, Asiana is in front of the Jeonju city-hall.

A : What is the best way to go there?

B : Please turn left at the Bank of Korea and go straight about 100 meters, then you will find it on the right side.

5 Role Play

Student A

A : 시내에 있는 호텔로 가는 버스 편 좀 가르쳐 주시겠습니까?

B : Bus? I think you mean limousine to take you to the hotel. To which hotel are you going?

A : 힐튼호텔입니다.

B : Then, you go out at that exit and wait for the limousine at the number two exit. The departure time is 9:15.

A : 표는 어디서 삽니까?

B : You can get one at that ticket booth or please pay the driver ten dollars.

A : 호텔까지 얼마나 걸립니까?

B : It takes about half an hour, but it depends on traffic.

A : 이 택시 운행합니까?

B : Yes, it is. Let me put your baggage here. Where are you going?

A : 파크 호텔까지 태워다 주세요.

B : Park Hotel. All right, sir.

A : 호텔까지 얼마나 걸립니까?

B : Normally, thirty minutes, but today the freeway is terribly congested. I'm afraid it will take twice as long.

A : 2배라고요?

B : Sorry... but I can't help it. Are you from Korea?

A : 예.

B : Koreans cars are very good. My brother bought a Hyndai Sonata last year.

A : 한국에 다녀오신 적이 있습니까?

B : Yes, I've been. I visited Seoul on a tour.

A : 아, 그러셨군요.

Student *B*

A : Would you tell me how to go to the hotel in the city by bus?

B : 버스요? 호텔로 가는 리무진을 말씀하시는 것 같군요. 어느 호텔로 가십니까?

A : Hilton Hotel.

B : 그러면, 저기 출구로 나가신 다음 2번 출구에서 리무진을 기다리세요. 출발 시간은 9시 15분입니다.

A : Where can I get a ticket?

B : 매표소에서 사시던가 아니면 운전기사에게 10달러를 지불하세요.

A : How long does it take to get to the hotel?

B : 약 30분 정도 걸리는데, 교통사정에 따라 다릅니다.

A : Is this taxi free?

B : 예, 그렇습니다. 이 짐은 여기에 놓겠습니다. 어디로 가십니까?

A : Please take me to the Park Hotel.

B : 파크 호텔요. 알겠습니다.

A : How long does it take to the Hotel?

B : 보통은 30분 걸립니다. 그러나 오늘은 고속도로가 매우 혼잡해서 시간이 약 2배 정도 걸릴 것 같습니다.

A : Twice as long?

B : 죄송합니다만, 어떻게 할 수가 없습니다. 한국에서 오셨습니까?

A : Yes.

B : 한국제 자동차는 매우 좋습니다. 제 동생은 지난 해 현대 소나타를 샀었습니다.

A : Have you been to Korea?

B : 예, 관광 삼아 서울에 다녀왔었습니다.

A : Oh, did you?

Unit 04 Check-in at the Hotel

1 Vocabulary and Patterns

* single bed 1인용 침대(90×195cm 이상)
  double bed 2인용 침대(138×195cm 이상)
  twin bed 1인용 침대 2개

객실의 종류(호텔서비스사 면접시험 문제)

Single Room / Double Room / Twin Room

Triple Room : Twin Room에 추가 침대 1개를 더 넣어 3인이 사용하는 객실

Suite Room : 침실(bed room)과 응접실(sitting room)이 따로 연결된 특실

Studio(Executive) Room : 침대로 전환되는 한 두 개의 긴 소파가 있는 침대가 없는 비즈니스호텔의 객실

Ondol Room : 온돌 방

* connecting room : 문으로 연결된 인접한 객실
  adjoining room : 연결문이 없는 인접한 객실

* blocking(blocked) room 단체손님이 예약해 놓은 객실로 미리 배정 해둔 객실

* out side room 외측 객실 / inside room 내측 객실
  vacant room 비어 있는 객실
  house use 호텔에서 공무로 이용하는 객실
* Out of Order Room 고장이 난 객실로 판매할 수 없는 객실

* room rate(charge) 객실요금 / room tariff 객실 요금표
  additional charge 12시 이후에 퇴실할 때 부과하는 초과요금
  off season rate 비수기 요금 / peak season rate 성수기 요금
  tax 세금 / service charges(SVC) 봉사료
  sub total 소계, total balance 합계

EX

A : A : What's the room rate?
B : $100.

호텔서비스사 자격증 면접시험 문제

* Bermuda Plan 미국식 조식이 포함된 객실요금
* Continental Plan 대륙식 조식이 포함된 객실요금
* Modified American Plan(MAP) 조식과 점심이나 저녁 중 하나가 포함된 객실요금
* Full American Plan(full pension, bed and board) 3식이 포함된 객실요금 - 1박 3식 제도
* European Plan(E.P) 식사가 포함되지 않은 객실요금
* doorman 호텔의 출 · 입객을 도와주는 사람
* bellman[bellhop] 손님의 짐을 객실까지 운반하고 정돈을 도와주는 종사원
* front desk 호텔 내에서 고객이 등록을 하거나 check-out하는 곳
* check-in 고객등록-고객의 영접 및 등록카드의 작성을 포함한 제반 입숙 절차
* check-out 회계정리 및 고객의 출발을 포함한 제반 퇴실 절차
* pre paid 체크아웃을 신속히 하기 위해 미리 요금을 정산
* room service 음식 및 음료의 객실 서비스

EX

안녕하십니까. 룸서비스입니다. 도와드릴까요? 호텔서비스사 면접
Good Morning. Room service speaking. May I help you?

* baggage[luggage] 여행 시 소지하는 개인 수하물
* group rooming list 단체 숙박 명부
* over booking 초과예약

호텔예약시의 기본 표현

I'd like to make a reservation. 예약하고 싶은데요.

I need a reservation for tonight. 오늘 밤 예약하려고 하는데요.

I need a reservation, please. A single. 예약하려고 하는데요. 1인용 객실로요.

I'm trying to make reservation for a large tour group.
대규모 여행단이 묵을 방을 예약하려고 하는데요.

What is your rate for a room with a king size bed?
킹사이즈 침대 하나가 들어 있는 방의 값이 얼마입니까?

How much do you charge for a room with two queen size bed?
퀸사이즈 침대 두 개가 들어 있는 방의 값이 얼마입니까?

I'd like a room near the pool.
수영장 근처에 있는 방이 좋겠는데요.

near the dining room.
식당 근처에

with a nice(good) view.
전망이 좋은

Exercise 1 ~을 예약하고 싶습니다.

I'd like to I want to	reserve ~ make a reservation for ~ book ~

Exercise 2 예약을 취소하고 싶습니다.

I'm sorry, I'm afraid,	I'd like to I've got to I want to I'm phoning to	cancel	my booking for ~ my reservation for ~

혹, 예약을 변경하고 싶을 때는 이름과 시간을 확인한 후
I'd like to change the date to ~라고 말하고, 반드시 변경사항을 확인하도록 한다.

2 Utterance-Response Drills

Hello. Ritz Hotel. May I help you?

I'd like to reserve a double room with a shower for the nights of March 6th to 10th.

One moment, please... Could you repeat the date, please?

Yes, from March 6th to 10th.

I'd like to book a single room with a shower, please.

When for, sir?

For the nights of July 10th to July 17th.

I'd like to find out the rate for two people for December 25th and 26th.

We have a holiday special. We give 20% off.

Wonderful, then I'd like to make reservations.

Hello. Red Lion Restaurant.

Hello. I want to reserve a table for tonight, at 8 o'clock.

Yes, sir. For how many people?

For six people.

May I have your name, please?

In the name of Lawrence.

Thank you, Mr. Lawrence. Goodbye.

This is Jane speaking. I want to cancel my reservation for two for tonight.

Can you repeat the name, please?

Jane. J-A-N-E.

Oh, yes. Thanks for letting us know, Miss Jane. Goodbye.

Excuse me, the airport information center recommended this hotel to me.
Yes, for course. Welcome to our hotel. Will that be a single or double room?
2 single rooms for 2 nights, please.

Good evening. Can I help you?
Yes, I' d like to check in, please. My name is Sang-jeong Bae. I have a reservation for three nights.
Just a moment, please. ... Oh, yes. One twin and one single. Is that right?
Yes, I' m with my wife and child.
Will you fill out this form, please.

I need a reservation for tonight.
How large is your party?
Two, please.
I can give you a double room with a nice view, sir.
Sounds great.

Beverly Hilton, reservations.
This is Yang-su Kim. I' d like to confirm my reservation.

I have a reservation and I know it' s late, but can I still check in?
I' ll see if we still have your room.

My English is not so good. Could you speak more slowly?
Of course.

Hello, we just arrived in L.A. Do you have any rooms?
I' m sorry, we' re booked solid.
Can you suggest another hotel?

3 Patterns Drill

(1) What kind of room would you like?
food
novel
movie
book

(2) How do you spell your surname?
given name
last name
family name
full name

(3) How long are you going to stay here?
I' m going to stay from June 6th to June 8th.
tonight tomorrow night.

(4) Are there any rooms available for tonight?
I' m sorry but we are booked up.
filled up
full up

4 Dialogue

Dialogue A

C : Reservation Clerk, G : Guest

C : Hilton Hotel reservation desk, Miss Green speaking.
May I help you?
힐튼호텔 예약실입니다. 저는 미스 그린입니다. 무엇을 도와드릴까요?

G : I' d like to reserve(get) a room.
Daeseong Travel Agency recommended your hotel to me.
객실을 예약하고 싶습니다. 대성 여행사에서 저에게 귀 호텔을 추천해 주었습니다.

C : May I have your name and phone number, please?
성함과 전화번호를 말씀해주시겠습니까?

G : Bae Sang-jeong, area code six three, phone number five three zero nine two nine one
제 이름은 배상정이고 전화번호는 지역번호 63, 전화번호 530-9291입니다.

C : How do you spell your surname?
당신의 성(姓)을 철자로 말씀해 주시겠습니까?

G : B-A-E

C : What kind of room would you like, sir?
어떤 종류의 객실을 원하십니까?

G : A single room, please.
싱글룸을 원합니다.

C : How long are you going to stay here?
얼마동안 머무실 예정입니까?

G : I' m going to stay from June 6th to June 8th.
6월 6일부터 8일까지 머물 예정입니다.

C : Thank you for calling.
전화해 주셔서 감사합니다.

Dialogue B

C : Shilla Hotel reservation desk. May I help you?
신라 호텔 예약창구입니다. 무엇을 도와드릴까요?

G : Are there any rooms(vacancies) available for tonight?
오늘밤 이용할 수 있는 객실이 있습니까?

C : I'm very sorry, sir. We're fully booked.
대단히 죄송합니다만, 모두 예약이 되었습니다.

G : Can you recommend any other hotel?
다른 호텔을 추천해 주실 수 있습니까?

C : Wait a moment, please. I'll try to call around for you.
잠시 기다리십시오. 주변 호텔에 전화해 보겠습니다.

Later 잠시 후

C : I'd like to recommend you to Holiday Inn.
손님께 Holiday Inn을 추천해 드립니다.

G : Thank you for your help.
도와주셔서 감사합니다.

사전에 예약을 하지 않았다면 객실을 구하기가 힘들지만 주변 호텔에 전화를 해서 객실이 남아 있는지를 먼저 확인하고, 만약 객실이 없으면 전화한 호텔에 다른 호텔을 추천해 달라고 부탁하면 대부분의 호텔에선 친절하게 안내해준다. 외국에서 Inn은 우리나라의 시설이 좋은 모텔급에 해당되고, Motel은 여관 정도의 시설이다.

유용한 표현들

I'm sorry but we are booked up.
I'm sorry but we are full up.(= we are filled up.)
죄송합니다만 모두 예약되었습니다.
That'd be great if you could find me a room.

Dialogue *C*

C : Good afternoon, sir. May I help you?
안녕하십니까? 손님, 무엇을 도와드릴까요?

G : Yes. I have a reservation for tonight. 예, 나는 오늘 밤 예약을 했습니다.

C : May I have your name, please? 성함을 말씀해 주시겠습니까?

G : My name is Gil-dong Hong. 제 이름은 홍길동입니다.

C : How do you spell your surname?
당신의 성(姓)을 철자로 말씀해 주시겠습니까?

G : H-O-N-G.

C : Yes, sir. A double room for two nights. Is that right?
예 손님, 2박에 더블룸이군요. 맞습니까?

G : That's right. 맞습니다.

C : Would you fill out this registration card, please?
이 등록 카드를 작성해 주시겠습니까?

G : Yes, here it is. 예, 여기 있습니다.

C : May I see your passport for a moment, please?
잠시 여권을 보여 주시겠습니까?

G : Yes, certainly. 예, 물론이지요.

C : Thank you, sir. Here's the key and the room number's 1812.
감사합니다, 손님. 열쇠를 받으시고, 객실 번호는 1812호입니다.

예약이 된 상태에서 호텔에 도착하면 Front Desk에서 등록을 하게 된다. 등록카드를 작성할 때에는 주소, 직업, 국적 등 개인 신상에 대해 영어로 기입해야 하고, 영문 성명 및 서명은 여권과 동일하게 해야 한다. 객실번호는 1812호일 경우 eighteen twelve로 두 자리씩 끊어서 말하면 된다.

Dialogue D

C : Good evening. May I help you, sir?
안녕하십니까. 손님 무엇을 도와드릴까요?

G : Yes. I have a reservation here for tonight.
예, 저는 오늘밤 이곳에 예약을 했습니다.

My name is Sang-jeong Bae. 제 이름은 배상정입니다.

C : Let me check. Wait a moment, please.
확인해보겠습니다. 잠시만 기다리십시오.

That was a double room. That's right? 더블룸이군요. 맞습니까?

G : Yes, that's right. 예, 맞습니다.

C : Would you fill out this registration card?
이 등록카드를 작성해 주시겠습니까?

How are you going to pay, sir? In cash or by credit card?
요금은 어떻게 지불하시겠습니까? 현금입니까? 신용카드입니까?

G : By credit card. 신용카드로 지불하겠습니다.

C : May I see your passport, please? 여권을 보여 주시겠습니까?

G : Yes, here it is. 예, 여기 있습니다.

C : Thank you, sir. Here's your key and the room number's 1812.
감사합니다 손님. 열쇠를 받으시고, 객실 번호는 1812호입니다.

The Bellman will show you to your room. Have a nice night.
벨맨이 객실까지 손님을 안내해 드릴 것입니다. 좋은 밤이 되시기를 바랍니다.

Front Desk에서 등록을 할 때 요금을 어떻게 지불하겠느냐고 질문을 받으면 현금일 경우 In cash, 신용카드일 경우 By credit card라고 대답하면 된다. 외국에선 신용카드를 사용하는 것이 보편화되어 있어 거리의 좌판에서도 신용카드를 받는다.

5 Role Play A

Student A

A : 안녕하세요! 어서 오십시오.

B : Yes. Do you have a room?

A : 예, 있습니다. 몇 분이시죠, 손님?

B : For two.

A : 킹사이즈 침대가 하나 들어있는 방이 있고, 퀸 사이즈 침대가 둘 있는 방이 있습니다.

B : How much do you charge for the room with a king size bed?

A : 95불입니다, 손님.

B : All right. I'll take the room with a king size bed.

A : 등록해 주시겠습니까?

B : OK. Do you accept credit cards?

A : 예. 마스터 와 비자카드를 받습니다. 크레디트 카드를 주시겠습니까?

B : Here it is.

A : 고맙습니다. 오늘만 묵으실 겁니까?

B : No, we'll take it for two days.

A : 좋습니다, 손님. 여기 열쇠 있습니다. 그리고 방 번호는 708호실입니다.

B : By the way, what is your check-out time?

A : 12시입니다.

B : How do I get to my room?

A : 엘리베이터가 바로 저기 있습니다. 짐은 우리가 방에 가져다 드립니다.

B : Thank you.

Student *B*

A : Hello! May I help you?

B : 예, 방이 있습니까?

A : Yes, we do. For how many people, sir?

B : 두 사람입니다.

A : We have rooms with a king size bed and rooms with two queen size beds, sir.

B : 킹사이즈 침대 하나가 들어있는 방은 얼마입니까?

A : Ninety five dollars, sir.

B : 좋습니다. 그 방에 들겠습니다.

A : Would you register for me, please?

B : 그러죠. 크레디트 카드를 받으세요.

A : Yes, sir. We accept Master and Visa. May I have your credit card?

B : 여기 있습니다.

A : Thank you, sir. Is this just for today?

B : 아닙니다, 이틀 있을 겁니다.

A : All right, sir. Here is your room key, and your room number is 708.

B : 참, 체크아웃 타임이 몇 시입니까?

A : It's twelve o'clock, sir.

B : 내 방엔 어떻게 가죠?

A : There is the elevator right over there. We'll take your luggage to your room, sir.

B : 감사합니다.

6 Role Play B

Student A

A : 좋은 아침입니다. 그랜드호텔입니다.

B : I'd like to reserve a double with shower, please.

A : 그러시죠. 날짜는요?

B : For April 12th and 13th.

A : 네, 가능합니다. 길가에 면한 방으로 원하십니까, 아니면 뒤쪽의 방을 원하십니까?

B : I would prefer a room on the street.

A : 어떤 분 앞으로 해놓을까요?

B : In the name of Yang Hi-yong. Can you tell me the price, please?

A : 하루에 95달러입니다.

A : 네, 첨블즈 레스토랑입니다.

B : Good morning. I'd like to book a table for the night of 16th of June at 8:30.

A : 좋습니다, 부인. 몇 분이시죠?

B : It's for two.

A : 성함을 대주시죠.

B : My name is Mrs. Song. Can you give me a quiet table, please?

A : 그럼요, 그렇게 준비해 드리겠습니다. 미세스 송. 그럼.

Student *B*

A : Good morning. Grand Hotel.

B : 샤워 시설이 된 더블룸 하나 예약하고 싶습니다.

A : Yes, certainly. For what date?

B : 4월 12일, 13 양일 간입니다.

A : Yes. That's all right. Do you want a room on the street or at the back?

B : 길가에 면한 방이 좋습니다.

A : In what name, please.?

B : 양희용 앞으로 해 주십시오. 숙박료를 알려 주시겠습니까?

A : That will be $95 per day.

A : Good morning. Chumble's Restaurant.

B : 네. 테이블 하나 예약하고 싶은데요. 6월 16일 밤 8시 30분입니다.

A : Certainly, ma'am. For how many?

B : 둘입니다.

A : And what is your name, please?

B : 미세스 송입니다. 조용한 자리로 주실 수 있죠?

A : Certainly, we'll arrange that Mrs. Song. Goodbye.

Unit 05

At the Hotel

1 Vocabulary and Patterns

* registration card 등록카드
* wake up call(=morning call) 손님이 원하는 시간에 깨워 주는 기상전화
* overseas call 국제전화
* extension 구내전화, 내선 / house phone 구내전화
* switchboard 교환대

* laundry 세탁물 / laundry slip 세탁물 전표
* temperature control 온도조절기 / thermostat 자동온도 조절장치

EX

호텔객실의 적절한 온도는? 호텔서비스사 면접
18℃~21℃(twenty one degrees centigrade)

* Do Not Disturb 방해하지 마시오-객실 입구 문고리에 걸어놓고 호텔 직원 등 외부인의 출입을 금하는 카드. 최근에는 플라스틱 카드 대신에 벽에 부착되어 있는 액정화면으로 교체되어 사용되고 있음.

* room maid 객실 청소를 담당하는 사람
  room inspector 객실 청소 상태를 점검하는 사람

bed making 침실을 꾸미는 일
on change room 청소가 필요한 객실

* key rack 객실열쇠를 보관하는 선반
(grand) master key 호텔의 모든 객실을 열 수 있는 키
pass key 층별로 구별하여 한 층에 있는 모든 객실을 열 수 있는 키
* lost and found 분실물 보관소 / safety box 귀중품 보관함

* emergency exit 비상구
* elevator(lift) 승강기

EX

Please watch your step while getting on the elevator.
승강기를 타실 때 조심하십시오.

* walk-in 사전에 예약을 하지 않고 입실하는 고객
sleeper 객실요금은 지불하였으나 투숙하지 않은 고객
skipper 계산을 하지 않고 몰래 빠져나가는 고객
no-show 예약을 하고 나타나지 않는 고객
Go-show 빈 객실을 기다리는 손님

* Guest History Card 고객관리카드
Room Assignment 객실배정
Daily Room Report 일일 객실 판매 보고서

* Night Auditor 야간 회계업무를 담당하는 회계원
Night Manager 당직지배인

호텔서비스사 자격증 면접시험 문제

* I.H.A(International Hotel Association) 국제호텔협회
  W.T.O(World Tourism Organization) 세계관광기구
  H.I.S(Hotel Information System) 호텔정보시스템
  P.O.S(Point of Sale) System 판매시점관리의 회계시스템

* 관광서비스의 3요소? Speed(신속), Smile(미소), Sincerity(성실)

EX

1. A : Christine, Hi. I ______ myself out. I don't know what to do.
   B : Oh! Why don't you call the locksmith we called last time? Do you want me to give you his number? He'll come right away.(TEPS)

   (a) put (b) took (c) left (d) locked

   I locked myself out = I'm locked out. 문이 잠겨 못 들어가다. locksmith 열쇠 수리공

2. A : Front desk. How can I help you?(중앙대 편입시험)
   B : Yes, I'd like to check out tomorrow. ______________

   (a) May I have your name, please?
   (b) Do you have anything available for tonight?
   (c) I'm going to the airport today.
   (d) Can you send a bellman to my room tomorrow morning?

★ 1. (d) 2.(d)

There is / There are
There is a/an **단수명사** ~. ~이/가 있다.
Is there a/an/any **단수명사** ~? ~이/가 있습니까?
There are (some) **복수명사** ~. ~들이 있다.
Are there any **복수명사** ~? ~들이 있습니까?

There are many different ways of greeting.
인사하는 방법도 가지가지입니다.

Should I shake hands or should I bow?
악수를 하는 게 좋을까요, 아니면 고개 숙여서 인사를 할까요?

Is there any pay phone around here?
여기 어디 공중전화 있나요?

Yes, it's in the rest room.
네, 화장실 안에 있습니다.

Excuse me. Is there a gas station nearby?
실례합니다. 이 근처에 주유소가 있습니까?

Yes. There's a gas station on Main Street, next to the supermarket.
예, 메인街, 슈퍼마켓 옆에 하나 있습니다.

2 Patterns Drill

(1) How do I call room service?

bellman

operator

Room 1234

(2) What time does the dining room open?

restaurant

gift shop

swimming pool

(3) The Television doesn't work.

refrigerator

air conditioner

lamp

3 Utterance-Response Drills

Room service.

I'd like to order a snack, please.

Can I order some champagne? This is the bridal suite.

I'll send it up right away.

Would you bring some ice and three glasses to room number 312?

Certainly, sir. I'll be there in ten minutes, sir.

Thank you.

My room number is 305. I think the light bulb in the bathroom has burned out. Please send a maintenance person right away.

OK, I'll send our engineer to your room.

What can I do for you? Are you in trouble?

I can't get in my room. I am locked out. Could you open the door for me?

Hello, I want to reserve a morning wake-up call.

What time?

Six o'clock tomorrow morning.

Your name and room number, please.

My name is Minho Kim and the room number is 715.

Six o'clock and room number is 715. All right, sir. Good night!

4 Dialogue

Dialogue A

C : Clerk, B : Bellman, G : Guest

C : Bellman! please take these bags to room 1812.
벨맨, 이 가방들을 1812호로 운반해 주세요.

B : Let me bring up your bags. 제가 가방을 운반해 드리겠습니다.

G : Yes, thank you. 예, 고맙습니다.

B : Please, come with me, and we'll take the elevator to your floor.
저와 함께 가시지요. 엘리베이터를 타고 손님이 투숙하실 객실층까지 가겠습니다.

The elevator door opens

B : Please watch your step when you get on the elevator.
승강기를 탈 때 조심해서 타십시오.

After arriving at room 1812.

B : Here's your room. Let me turn on the light and open the curtains for you. The temperature control is on the wall.
이곳이 손님이 사용하실 객실입니다. 전등을 켜고 커튼을 열어 드리겠습니다. 온도조절기는 벽에 부착되어 있습니다.

Please call me if you need any help.
만약 다른 도움이 필요하시면 저를 불러주십시오.

G : Thank you. Here's something for you. 고맙습니다. 팁을 받으세요.

B : Thank you. Have a nice day. 감사합니다. 좋은 하루 되십시오.

Front Desk에서 등록을 한 후 Bellman이 짐을 객실까지 운반해 주는 과정이다. 짐을 운반해 준 벨맨에게 적당한 팁을 주는 것이 상례이고, 벨맨을 통해서 객실 내 온도조절기의 위치와 사용법, 취침등의 스위치 등은 사전에 꼭 숙지하는 것이 필요하다. 여름철엔 취침 중에 객실온도가 너무 내려가 감기에 걸리는 경우가 많으니 취침 전에 적당한 온도로 조정을 해놓는 것이 필요하다.

Dialogue *B*

H : Housekeeper, G : Guest

H : Housekeeping, may I help you? 하우스 키핑입니다, 무엇을 도와드릴까요?

G : I'd like to have one more blanket. 담요 한 장이 더 필요합니다.

H : May I have your room number? 객실번호가 어떻게 되십니까?

G : Room 1812. 1812호실입니다.

H : Do you need anything else? 더 필요하신 것이 있으십니까?

G : My room is not cold enough. 객실이 시원하지가 않습니다.

H : There is an air conditioning controller on the wall.
벽에 에어컨 조절기가 있는데요.

G : It is still warm even though I adjusted it lower.
낮게 조정을 했는데도 여전히 덥습니다.

H : Something seems to be wrong. I will report it to the maintenance department and have it fixed immediately.
고장인 것 같습니다. 수선부에 보고해서 즉시 수선하도록 하겠습니다.

G : Thank you. 고맙습니다.

객실을 사용하는 중에 필요로 하는 물품이 있을 경우 하우스키핑에 연락을 하면 가져다준다. 담요, 타월 등은 무료로 빌려주고 비누, 삼푸 등의 일회용품은 추가로 필요할 경우 무료로 제공하므로 하우스키핑에 연락을 하면 된다. 객실 내 TV나 비품 등이 고장인 경우 수선부(maintenance department)에 연락을 하면 되고, 문제가 있는데 담당 부서의 전화번호를 모르면 프런트 데스크로 연락을 해도 해결할 수 있다. 냉방기는 우리나라에서만 에어컨으로 발음하므로 외국에서는 에어컨디셔너(air conditioner)로 발음해야 한다.

Dialogue *C*

R : Room Service Clerk, G : Guest

R : Room Service, may I help you? 룸서비스입니다, 무엇을 도와드릴까요?

G : **Yes, I' d like to reserve breakfast for two.**
예, 조식 2인분을 주문하고 싶습니다.

R : May I take your order now? 지금 주문하시겠습니까?

G : **I can' t find a menu.** 메뉴판을 찾을 수 없군요.

R : You' ll find a menu in the desk drawer, sir. 책상 서랍 속에 있습니다.

G : **Oh, wait a moment, ... I' ve found the menu. Please bring me orange juice, two eggs, bread and butter and coffee.**
아, 잠시만 기다리십시오, 메뉴판을 찾았습니다. 오렌지 주스, 계란 2인분, 버터 바른 빵과 커피를 가져다 주세요.

R : How would you like your eggs? 계란은 어떻게 요리해 드릴까요?

G : **Sunny side up, please.** 한 쪽 면만 익혀주세요.

R : What time would you like it served, sir? 손님 몇 시에 가져다 드릴까요?

G : **How long will it take?** 시간이 얼마나 걸립니까?

R : Your order will be up in about 20 minutes. 약 20분 후면 준비될 것입니다.

G : **At 8:30.** 8시 30분에 가져다 주세요.

R : Yes, sir. May I have your name and room number?
알겠습니다, 손님. 성함과 객실번호를 말씀해 주시겠습니까?

G : **This is Mr. Bae in room 1234.** 1234호실의 미스터 배입니다.

객실에서 식사를 하거나 음료 및 술등을 먹고 싶을 때는 룸서비스를 신청하면 된다. 메뉴판은 대부분 객실 내 책상 위나 서랍 안에 있으니 참고하여 주문하면 된다. 계란을 주문할 때는 노른자가 그대로 있는 프라이를 원하면 sunny side up, please. 앞뒤로 반쯤만 익힌 것은 over easy. 양면을 완전히 익힌 것은 turned over.라고 말하면 된다. bread and butter는 빵과 버터가 아니라 버터를 발라 구운 빵을 말하며 음성작용에 의하여 『브레든 버러』로 발음해야 한다.

Dialogue *D*

L : Laundry Clerk, G : Guest

L : Laundry service, may I help you?
세탁 서비스입니다, 무엇을 도와드릴까요?

G : Yes, I'd like to have my shirt cleaned and pressed.
Can you send someone over to my room?
예, 저는 셔츠를 드라이클리닝하고 싶습니다. 제 방으로 누구를 좀 보내주시겠습니까?

L : May I have your name and room number, please?
성함과 객실번호를 말씀해주시겠습니까?

G : This is Mr. Bae in room 1234.
1234호실의 미스터 배입니다.

L : All right, sir. I'll send a valet to your room.
좋습니다, 손님. 직원을 방으로 보내드리겠습니다.

G : When will my shirt be delivered?
셔츠는 언제 배달해주나요?

L : We will deliver it by tomorrow morning.
내일 아침까지는 배달됩니다.

G : Ok, thank you.
좋습니다, 감사합니다.

세탁이 필요한 세탁물이 있을 때는 세탁서비스를 신청하면 된다. 세탁물을 보이에게 맡길 때 작성해야 할 세탁물 전표(Laundry Slip)는 대부분 옷장 안에 있다. 빨리 세탁을 해야 할 때는 50% 정도의 추가요금(extra charge)을 지불하면 가능하고, 세탁요금은 우리나라 세탁소 요금보다 비싸다.

Dialogue *E*

C : Clerk, G : Guest

G : Where can I cash traveller's checks? 수표를 어디에서 바꿀 수 있습니까?

C : **Go to the 1st floor in this hotel.** 이 호텔의 1층으로 가십시오.

G : I want to cash this traveler's check.
이 여행자 수표를 현금으로 바꾸고 싶습니다.

C : **O.K. How much do you want to exchange?**
좋습니다, 얼마나 바꾸시겠습니까?

G : Two hundred dollars, please. 200달러입니다.

C : **Here you are.** 여기 있습니다.

G : Can I have a ten, a five and five ones for this twenty?
이 20달러를 10달러 1장, 5달러 1장, 1달러 5장으로 바꾸어 주시겠습니까?

C : **Certainly sir. Here it is.** 물론이지요, 손님. 여기 있습니다.

G : One more thing, please. Can I break a dollar into some small coins? 한 가지 더 있는데요. 1달러를 동전으로 바꾸어 주시겠습니까?

C : **Certainly sir. Will 3 quarters, 2 dimes and a nickel do?**
물론이지요. 25센트 3개, 10센트 2개, 5센트 동전 1개면 되겠습니까?

G : Yes, thank you very much. 예, 대단히 감사합니다.

외국 공항이나 호텔에 도착해서 여행자 수표를 현금으로 바꾸거나, 지폐를 동전으로 바꾸는 경우가 있다. 공항의 환전소에서 돈을 바꾸지 못했을 경우 호텔 로비에 있는 환전소를 이용하면 된다. 지폐를 이야기할 때 10달러 1장은 a ten, 2장은 two tens라고 말하며 5달러 4장은 four fives라고 표현한다. 동전은 공중전화나 카지노에서 사용하는 25¢짜리 a quarter, 10¢짜리 a dime, 5¢짜리 a nickel, 1 cent짜리 a penny, 50 cents짜리 a half dollar가 있다.

유용한 표현들

How would you like to have the money? 돈을 어떻게 바꾸어 드릴까요?
I would like have small money as much as possible.
가능한 작은 돈으로 바꾸어 주세요.

Dialogue *F*

C : Clerk, G : Guest

G : Where can I change some money? 어디에서 환전을 할 수 있습니까?

C : Go to the 1st floor in this hotel. 이 호텔의 1층으로 가십시오.

G : I'd like to exchange dollars to Thailand baht(THB), what's the exchange rate? 달러를 바트로 바꾸고 싶은데 환율이 어떻게 됩니까?

C : It's 29 baht to a dollar. How much do you want to exchange?
1달러에 29바트입니다. 얼마나 바꾸시겠습니까?

G : Two hundred dollars, please. 200달러입니다.

C : Here you are. 여기 있습니다.

G : Thank you very much. 대단히 감사합니다.

우리나라 은행이나 공항 환전소에서 미국(달러), 일본(엔), 영국(파운드), 독일(마르크), 캐나다(달러), 프랑스(프랑), 이태리(리라), 스위스(프랑), 홍콩(달러), 스웨덴(크로나), 호주(달러), 덴마크(크로네), 네덜란드(길더), 사우디(리알), 싱가포르(달러), 태국(바트), 스페인(패세라), 핀란드(마르카), EU(유로화) 등은 현지화폐로 환전을 할 수 있지만 그 밖의 나라들은 미국 달러로 환전을 한 후 현지에서 그 나라의 원화로 다시 바꾸어 사용해야 한다. 면세점이나 큰 백화점 등에서는 신용카드나 미달러를 많이 사용하지만 조그만 상점 등에서는 현지화폐를 사용하므로 호텔 환전소에서 현지 화폐를 쓸 만큼 바꾸어 놓는 것이 필요하다.

유용한 표현들

Could you break(change)a twenty dollar bill?
= Do you have change for a twenty?
= Could I have change for a twenty?
20달리싸리 지폐를 바꾸어 주시겠습니까?

I would like have small money as much as possible.
가능한 작은 돈으로 바꾸어 주세요.

5 Role Play

Student A

A : 식당설비로는 무엇 무엇이 있습니까?

B : Our coffee shop is next to that lounge, and it's open from six o'clock till eleven o'clock in the morning. And, the main dining room is on the top floor. We also have a night club way in the back on this floor.

A : 나이트클럽은 몇 시에 문을 엽니까?

B : Dinner starts at seven o'clock and the show starts at nine.

A : 이 부근에 동양 음식점이 있어요?

B : There are a lot of Japanese restaurants on 3rd Street, and Chinatown is not too far from here.

A : 한국 음식점은 없어요?

B : Oh, yes. There are many Korean restaurants on 8th Street.

A : 거기까지 걸어갈 수 있어요?

B : No, sir. Depending on where you are going, it will take 15 or 20 minutes by car.

B : Room service. Can I help you?

A : 예, 내일 아침 식사를 주문하고 싶은데요.

B : What do you want to have for breakfast?

A : 토마토주스, 스크램블드에그, 베이컨과 커피를 먹고 싶습니다.

B : What time shall we bring our breakfast, sir?

A : 7시에 부탁드립니다.

B : What is your name and room number?

A : 1518호실, 홍길동입니다.

B : Thank you, and is this only for you?

A : 물론이죠, 제 식사입니다.

Student *B*

A : Could you tell me what kind of eating facilities you have?

B : 커피숍은 저 라운지 옆에 있는데, 아침 6시부터 11시까지 엽니다. 그리고 식당은 맨 윗층에 있습니다. 그리고 나이트클럽도 있는데 본 층의 저 뒤에 있습니다.

A : What time does the night club open?

B : 저녁 식사는 7시에 시작하고 쇼는 9시에 시작합니다.

A : Are there any oriental restaurants nearby?

B : 3街에 일본 음식점이 많고 중국 거리가 여기서 멀지 않습니다.

A : Are there any Korean restaurants?

B : 아, 예. 8번가에 한국 음식점이 많습니다.

A : Can we walk there?(or Are they within walking distance?)

B : 아닙니다. 어디로 가시느냐에 따라 다르지만, 대략 자동차로 15분 내지 20분 걸립니다.

B : 룸서비스입니다. 도와드릴까요?

A : Yes, I want to have breakfast tomorrow morning.

B : 무엇을 드시겠습니까?

A : I'd like to have tomato juice, scrambled eggs, with bacon and coffee.

B : 아침 식사를 몇 시에 가져갈까요?

A : At seven, please.

B : 성함과 방 번호를 말씀해 주십시오.

A : GIL-DONG HONG. Room 1518.

B : 감사합니다. 그런데 일인분이지요?

A : Of course, it's for myself.

Unit 06

Asking directions(I)

1 Vocabulary and Patterns

길 묻기(Asking directions)

비격식체

Excuse me.	Which way is	목적지
Pardon me.	How do I get to	

격식체

Excuse me.	Would you know	how to get to 목적지?
	Could you tell me	where 목적지 is?

방향 및 위치 표현

Go(straight)	down up	this street 거리 명	about two blocks. to until you come to and you' ll find	거리 명 건물 명

It' s	(on the left/right) next to (just) past / before opposite / across from	기준 건물 명 장소 명
	on the corner in the middle of the book	on your left on your right

2 Patterns Drill

(1) Can you tell me how to get to the airport?
post office
restaurant
city hall

(2) I' m new in Seoul.
around here
a stranger here
get lost on the way

(3) How far is it from here?
from Seoul to Busan
from here to Gyeongju
from this hotel to airport

(4) Go straight ahead.
up
across the front desk
the street

3 Utterance-Response Drills

Excuse me. Which way is the post office?

Go up this street. It's on the left next to the drugstore.

Excuse me. How do I get to the Plaza Hotel?

Go straight down this street to the end of the block. It's on the corner on your left.

Excuse me. Could you tell me where the police station is?

The police station? Uh, let me think for a moment. Ah, yes. It's down this street about two blocks.

Thank you very much.

You're welcome.

Excuse me. Would you know how to get to the Shopping Center?

Go down this street for two blocks until you come to the high school. Make a left and go two blocks more. Cross the street, and it's at the end of the block just across from the library.

Excuse me, I'm lost. Can you direct me to the Central Hotel?

the Central Hotel? Sorry, I don't know.

Well, thanks anyway.

Excuse me, I'm trying to find a pay phone. Can you help me?

Okay, just follow me. I'm going that way, so I'll show you.

4 Dialogue

Dialogue A

D : Driver T : Tourist

D : Where (are you going) to, sir? 손님, 어디까지 가십니까?

T : (I' m going to the) Hilton Hotel. 힐튼호텔까지 갑니다.

D : Let me load your bags. 가방을 싣겠습니다.

Later 잠시 후

T : Are we there, yet? 다와 갑니까?

D : Almost. 거의 요.

A few minutes late 몇 분 후

D : Here we are, sir. 다 왔습니다.

T : Oh, How much is it? 아, 요금이 얼마죠?

D : $ 18.50, sir. 18달러 50센트입니다.

T : Here you go. Keep the change. 여기 있습니다. 거스름돈은 그냥 가지세요.

D : Thank you , sir. 고맙습니다, 손님

공항에서 호텔로 이동하거나, 호텔에서 가고자 하는 목적지까지 택시를 이용하는 경우가 있다. 택시를 타기 전, 후 목적지를 이야기할 때 (Can you) take me to Hilton Hotel? (힐튼호텔까지 가주실 수 있습니까?)라고 말하면 되고, 일행이 있을 경우 Take us to 목적지. 라고 말하면 된다. 내릴 때에는 대부분 택시요금의 10% 정도를 팁으로 주면 되는데 거스름돈이 10% 정도 남을 때는 Keep the change라고 말하면 된다. 장거리 경우에는 요금이 얼마 정도 나오는지를 미리 물어보고 타는 것이 현명하다.

Dialogue *B*

P : Passerby, T : Tourist

T : Where is the nearest bus stop?
가장 가까운 버스 정류장이 어디에 있습니까?

P : Turn right at the next corner. 다음 모퉁이에서 우회전하십시오

T : Thank you. 고맙습니다.

Later 잠시 후

T : Can I take a shuttle bus to downtown from here?
이곳에서 시내까지 가는 셔틀버스를 탈 수 있습니까?

P : Yes, you can. 예, 탈 수 있습니다.

T : How long does it take to get downtown by bus?
버스로 시내까지 시간이 얼마나 걸립니까?

P : (It takes) about fifty minutes, it depends on traffic conditions.
약 50분 정도 소요됩니다만, 교통상황에 따라 다릅니다.

T : How often does it run? 버스는 몇 분마다 운행합니까?

P : Every half an hour. 30분 간격으로 있습니다.

T : How much is it? 요금은 얼마입니까?

P : Three dollars. 3달러입니다.

공항에서 호텔로 이동하거나, 호텔에서 가고자 하는 목적지까지 버스를 이용하는 경우가 있다. 버스를 타기 전에 주변 버스 정류장의 위치, 소요시간, 요금 등을 미리 알아두면 편하게 이용할 수 있다. 여행하는 나라의 지리를 잘 모를 경우 택시를 이용하는 것이 편리하기는 하지만, 버스를 이용하면 그 나라 시민들의 교통문화를 몸소 체험할 수 있어 정감 어린 여행 경험을 할 수 있다. bus stop을 발음할 때에는(버스 스탑)이 아니고 묵음작용에 의하여(버스 탑)으로 발음해야 한다. 주유소를 발음할 때도 gas station(게 스테이션)으로 발음하는 것과 같은 규칙이다.

유용한 표현들

Each has a number.

버스마다 노선 번호가 있습니다.

The number indicates their final destination.

노선 번호는 버스의 최종 목적지를 표시합니다.

Most hotels provide shuttle bus service from airport to their hotel.

대부분 호텔들은 공항에서 호텔까지 셔틀버스 서비스를 제공합니다.

Dialogue *C*

P : Passerby, T : Tourist

T : Where is the nearest subway station?
가장 가까운 지하철역이 어디에 있습니까?

P : Turn right at the next corner and you'll see the entrance to the subway station. Are you new in this city?
다음 모퉁이에서 우회전하시면 지하철역 입구가 보입니다. 이 도시에 처음이십니까?

T : Yes, I am. 예, 그렇습니다.

P : What station are you going to. 어떤 역까지 가십니까?

T : I need to get off at City Hall stop. 시청역에서 내려야 합니다.
How long does it take to get to City Hall stop by subway?
지하철로 시청역까지 시간이 얼마나 걸립니까?

P : (It takes) about thirty minutes 약 30분 정도 소요됩니다.

T : How often does it run? 지하철은 몇 분 간격으로 운행됩니까?

P : Every three minutes. 3분 간격으로 있습니다.

T : How much is it? 요금은 얼마입니까?

P : Two dollars. 2달러입니다.

호텔에서 가고자 하는 목적지까지 지하철을 이용하는 경우가 있다. 지하철을 타기 전에 주변 지하철역의 위치, 소요시간, 요금 등을 미리 알아두면 편하게 이용할 수 있다. 여행하는 나라의 지리를 잘 모를 경우 택시를 이용하는 것이 편리하기는 하지만, 지하철을 이용하면 그 나라 시민들의 교통문화를 몸소 체험할 수 있다. 버스 정류장을 bus stop이라고 하는 것처럼 지하철역도 역 이름 뒤에 stop을 붙여 말하면 된다.

5 Role Play

Student A

A : 실례합니다. 저는 Wall 街 708번지를 찾고 있습니다. 그곳이 어딘지 말씀해 주시겠어요?

B : Sorry, I'm not sure. I'm a stranger in this city. You could ask that police officer standing there.

A : 감사합니다.

A : 실례합니다. 경찰 아저씨, 저는 이 명함에 적힌 주소를 찾고 있습니다.

B : Wait a moment. I'll look on the map of this district. Oh, here it is. It's quite close. You see that barber shop over there? The house you are looking for is right behind it.

A : 대단히 감사합니다.

B : You're welcome.

A : 저 실례합니다. 저는 씨티은행을 찾으려고 하는데요. 도와주시겠어요?

B : Citi Bank? Let's see now. Oh, yes. You go straight down this street to the corner. Turn left and go one block until you come to Broadway. Go right on Broadway. It's on the right side of the street just past the grocery store. You can't miss it.

A : 알겠습니다. 곧장 저 모퉁이로 가서 왼쪽으로 돌아서 그리고 오른쪽으로.

B : That's right.

A : 대단히 고맙습니다.

B : You're very welcome.

Student *B*

A : Excuse me, I'm looking for 708 Wall Street. Could you tell me where that is?

B : 미안합니다. 모르겠는데요. 저는 이 도시 사람이 아니어서 지리를 잘 모릅니다. 저기 서 있는 저 경찰관에게 물어보시지요.

A : Thank you.

A : Excuse me, officer. I'm trying to locate the address on this card.

B : 잠깐만 기다리세요. 제가 이 지역의 지도에서 찾아보겠습니다. 아, 바로 여기로군요. 아주 가깝습니다. 저기 저 이발소 보이시죠? 당신이 찾고 있는 그 집은 바로 저 이발소 뒤에 있습니다.

A : Thank you so much.

B : 천만에요.

A : Uh, excuse me. I'm trying to find Citi Bank. Can you help me?

B : 씨티은행요? 가만 있어보자. 아, 예. 이 길로 곧장 내려가 모퉁이가 나오면 왼쪽으로 돌아서 한 블록 더 가세요. 그러면 브로드웨이가 나옵니다. 브로드웨이 길을 타고 오른쪽으로 가세요. 식료품가게 바로 지나 도로 오른편에 있습니다. 찾기 쉽습니다.

A : I see. Straight to the corner. Left and then right.

B : 맞습니다.

A : Thanks a lot.

B : 천만에요.

Unit 07
Asking directions(Ⅱ)

1 Vocabulary and Patterns

위치 · 방향 묻기

① Is there a place near here where I can~?
이 근처에 ~ 할 수 있는 곳이 있습니까?

② Where's the nearest bus stop?
가장 가까운 버스정류장은 어디입니까?

Where is the subway station around here?
이 근처 지하철역은 어디입니까?

Where do I get the bus for City Hall?
시청 행 버스는 어디에서 탑니까?

* gas station 주유소 / bus station(stop) 버스 정류장
train station(stop) 역

EX

I have to stop at a gas station on my way home.
나는 집에 가는 길에 주유소에 들러야 한다.

A : Do you know where the nearest gas _______ is?
B : Sure. If you turn on the left at the end of this street, there is one on your right.(TEPS Voca Part I)

(a) store (b) station (c) shop (d) stop

③ Which bus do I take to get to Wall Street?
월스트리트에 가려면 어떤 버스를 타야 합니까?

Which station should I change at?
어떤 역에서 갈아 타야 합니까?

Which floor is the camera shop on?
어떤 층에 카메라 가게가 있죠?

④ Is this the right direction for Seoul Station?
서울역으로 가는 길이 여기가 맞습니까?

Is this bus bound for the airport?
이 버스는 공항으로 갑니까?

Does this bus go to Kennedy Center?
이 버스 케네디 센터로 갑니까?

2 Utterance-Response Drills

Is there a place around here where I can buy some souvenirs?

Yes, there's a shop at the end of the corridor.

Excuse me. I'm looking for Citi Bank.

Citi Bank? Let me think now. Oh, yes. It's on Fox Street.

Is that the street that's parallel to Broadway?

No, it's parallel to Hill.

Which floor is the toy department on?

It's upstairs, on the third floor.

Excuse me.

Yes, can I help you?

Is there a bus tour that can show us this city's sightseeing spots in about half a day?

Hum, okay. This will be fine. When does it leave?

It leaves at one o'clock from the bus stop in front of the station. The cost is $10.

I see. Could I have a pamphlet?

Of course. Here you are.

What's the quickest way to go there?

By subway.

Oh, is that right? Is there a subway station near here?

Yes, there's one on the other side of the building.

3 Dialogue

Dialogue A

T : Tourist, P : Passerby

T : Excuse me. 실례합니다.

P : Can I help you? 도와드릴까요?

T : Yes, What's the best way to get to the Empire State Building?
예, Empire State 빌딩에 갈 수 있는 가장 좋은 방법은 무엇입니까?

P : It's a lot more convenient to take the bus.
버스를 타시는 것이 훨씬 편해요.

T : Can I get a bus around here? 이 근처에서 버스를 탈 수 있습니까?

P : Yes, you can. 예, 탈 수 있습니다.

T : How long does it take to get to the Empire State Building by bus?
버스로 엠파이어 스테이트 빌딩까지 가는데 시간이 얼마나 걸립니까?

P : (It takes) about twenty minutes 약 20분 정도 소요됩니다.

T : Where is the nearest bus stop?
가장 가까운 버스 정류장이 어디에 있습니까?

P : It's at the end of this block. 이 블록 끝에 있습니다.

T : Thank you very much. 대단히 감사합니다.

여행 중 가고자 하는 목적지까지 이동하기 위해서는 가장 빠르고 편리한 교통수단을 현지인에게 문의하는 것이 필요하다. 미국 도시 내에서 이동할 때는 지하철(subway)이 운행되는 대도시를 제외하고는 대부분 시내버스(city bus)를 이용한다. 버스는 타기 전에 주변 버스 정류장의 위치, 소요시간, 요금 등을 미리 알아두면 편하게 이용할 수 있으며, 미국의 시내버스도 우리나라처럼 안내원 없이 운전사 혼자 운행함으로 미리 잔돈을 준비해야 한다.

Dialogue *B*

T : Tourist, P : Passerby

T : Excuse me.
실례합니다.

P : Can I help you?
도와드릴까요?

T : Yes, which bus goes to Central Park?
예, 센트럴 공원까지 가는 버스가 몇 번입니까?

P : Take number 22. It' ll take you there.
22번을 타십시오. 그 버스가 그곳에 갈 겁니다.

T : How often does it run on this route?
이 노선의 버스는 얼마 간격으로 운행됩니까?

P : (There' s a bus) every twenty minutes.
20분 간격으로 있습니다.

Later 잠시 후

T : Does this bus stop at Central Park?
센트럴 공원 앞에서 섭니까?

D : Yes, get on, please.
예, 타십시오.

버스를 타기 전에 현지인에게 가고자 하는 목적지의 버스 노선 번호를 물어 보는 것이 필요하다. 승차해야 할 버스의 운행 간격을 알고 싶을 때는 How often does it run on this route?(이 노선의 버스는 얼마 간격으로 운행됩니까?)라고 질문하며, 버스를 타기 전에는 Does this bus stop at+목적지?(목적지 앞에서 섭니까?)라고 물어본 후에 타는 것이 현명하다.

Dialogue *C*

D : Driver, T : Tourist

D : Where to, sir?
손님, 어디까지 가십니까?

T : Downtown, please.
시내까지 갑니다.

D : What part of downtown are you going to?
시내 어느 지역으로 가십니까?

T : 5th Avenue.
5번가입니다.

A few minutes late　몇 분 후

D : Here we are, sir.
다 왔습니다.

T : Oh, how much is the fare?
아, 요금이 얼마입니까?

D : 13 dollars, sir.
13달러입니다.

T : Here you are. Keep the change, please
여기 있습니다. 거스름돈은 가지세요.

D : Thank you , sir.
고맙습니다, 손님

미국 뉴욕의 경우 택시 색깔이 노란색이어서 Yellow Cab이라고 부르며, 요금 산정 방법은 구역제(zone system)와 거리제(mileage system) 두 가지로 주마다 다르다. 내릴 때는 대부분 택시요금의 10~15% 정도를 팁으로 주면 되는데 거스름돈이 10% 정도 남을 때는 Keep the change라고 말하면 된다.

Dialogue *D*

Y : Yellow Cab, T : Tourist

Y : This is Yellow Cab. May I help you?
택시회사입니다. 무엇을 도와드릴까요?

T : I need a ride to Kennedy Airport at 2 p.m this afternoon. Could you send me a taxi?
저는 오늘 오후 2시에 케네디공항까지 가야 되는데, 택시 좀 보내주시겠습니까?

Y : Sure. Where shall we pick you up?
물론이지요. 어디로 모시러 가면 되겠습니까?

T : In front of the Hilton Hotel at 2 o' clock sharp.
2시 정각에 힐튼호텔 앞으로 와 주세요.

Y : All right. And your name, please.
알겠습니다. 성함이 어떻게 되십니까?

T : Bae. B-A-E. 배입니다.

Y : Ok, Mr. Bae. We'll be there at two.
알겠습니다, 미스터 배. 2시에 모시러 가겠습니다.

호텔 현관에서 택시를 타는 경우도 있지만 시간에 맞추어 공항 등에 갈 때에는 미리 택시를 예약해 놓는 것이 필요하다. 택시를 부르려면 전화번호 책의 Yellow Pages(노란 종이)에서 Taxicabs라고 써 놓은 곳을 찾아보면 택시회사의 이름과 전화번호가 나온다. 객실 내에 전화번호부 책이 없을 경우에는 Front Desk나 Doorman에게 전화하여 콜택시를 부탁해도 된다.

4 Role Play

Student A

A : 실례지만, 아가씨. 와이셔츠 파는 데가 어디죠?

B : Take the elevator to the fifth floor.

A : 엘리베이터는 어디에 있습니까?

B : Turn left and it's right around the corner.

A : 고맙습니다.

B : Have a good time shopping.

A : 안녕하세요, 브라운 박사님 안에 계십니까?

B : He's in class now, but he'll be out at three o'clock. Have a seat, please. He'll be with you in a moment.

A : 그런데, 베이커 박사님 사무실은 어디에 있는지 아십니까?

B : No, I think you should check at the information desk.

A : 고마워요. 나중에 물어보겠습니다. 저- , 화장실이 어디에 있는지 가리켜 주시겠어요?

B : I beg your pardon?

A : 화장실이 어디 있냐고요.

B : Go out the door and take a left.

A : 잠깐 실례하겠습니다. 곧 돌아오겠습니다.

B : That's all right. Please go ahead.

Student 𝓑

A : Pardon me, miss. Where can I buy white shirts?

B : 승강기를 타고 5층으로 가세요?

A : Where can I find the elevator?

B : 왼쪽으로 돌면 바로 그 모퉁이에 있습니다.

A : Thank you.

B : 즐거운 쇼핑하세요.

A : Hello, is Dr. Brown in?

B : 그는 지금 강의 중입니다. 그러나 3시에는 강의가 끝나실 것입니다. 좀 앉으시죠. 잠시 후면 그분을 만나실 수 있을 거예요.

A : By the way, do you know where Dr. Baker's office is?

B : 모르겠는데요. 저 안내소에 물어보시지요.

A : Thank you. I'll try there later. Well, could you tell me where I can wash my hands?

B : 무엇이라고 말씀하셨나요?

A : I want to wash my hands.

B : 문 밖으로 나가서 왼쪽으로 도세요.

A : Excuse me. I'll be back soon.

B : 좋습니다. 그렇게 하십시오.

Unit 08

Shopping(I)

1 Vocabulary and Patterns

How many ~? / How much ~?

How many (복수명사)	are + 주어 ~ ?
	do + 주어 + 타동사원형 ~ ?

How many hotels are there in this city? 몇 개의 호텔이 이 도시에 있습니까?

How many do you want? 당신은 몇 개(또는 몇 명)를 원하십니까?

How much(불가산명사)	is/are + 주어 ~ ?
	does/do + 주어 + 타동사원형 ~ ?

How much money do you have? 돈은 얼마나 가지고 있습니까?

How much do you want? 얼마만큼 원하시지요?

가격 또는 비용을 묻는 표현

How much is 단수주어 / are 복수주어 ?
How much does 단수주어 / do 복수주어 cost ?
How much do you pay for 물건 ?
How much is it to 동사원형 ~ ?
How much does it cost to 동사원형 ~ ?
How much do you pay to 동사원형 ~ ?

2 Patterns Drill

(1) May I help you?
Can

(2) What size do you wear?
need
like
want

(3) I' m a small size.
medium
large
an average

(4) May I try on this dress?
shirt
coat
cap

(5) I' m just looking around.
browsing through

3 Utterance-Response Drills

How many children do you have?

I have two.

How many cups of coffee do you drink a day?

I drink three cups of coffee a day.

How much water do you drink a day?

I drink about five glasses of water a day.

How much money did you spend at the restaurant last night?

I spent thirty dollars.

How much is this book?

It's $17.

How much does the computer cost?

It is $6,000 to buy that.

How much is it to buy that?

It costs about $1,000.

How much did you pay for your CD-ROM drive?

I paid $340.

4 Dialogue

Dialogue A

S : Sales women, G : Guest

S : Are you looking for some souvenirs? 기념품을 찾고 계십니까?

G : **Yes, I am. What kind of souvenirs do you have to take to Korea?**
예, 그렇습니다. 한국에 가지고 갈 기념품으로는 어떤 종류가 있습니까?

S : For typical souvenirs, I recommend English tea, a rain coat, chinaware or something like that.
대표적인 기념품으로 영국산 홍차, 우의, 도자기 등을 권해 드리고 싶군요.

G : **Which of them do you recommend for me?**
그 중 어떤 물건이 좋겠습니까?

S : English tea is what many tourists take an interest in as souvenirs.
기념품으로 많은 관광객들이 선호하는 것은 영국산 홍차입니다.

G : **How much is this one?** 이것은 얼마입니까?

S : 20 dollars. 20불입니다.

G : **Do you have a cheaper one?** 더 싼 것은 없습니까?

S : This is $10 per set. 이것은 세트 당 10불입니다.

G : **Oh, this seems good. I' ll take it.** 이게 좋을 것 같네요. 이것을 사겠습니다.

G : All right, sir. 좋습니다, 손님

물건을 고른 후 가격을 물어 볼 때는 How much(does it cost)?/ How much do I owe you? / How much is this one?(이것은 얼마입니까?)라고 말하면 된다.

Dialogue *B*

S : Sales women, G : Guest

S : May I help you?
도와드릴까요?

G : Yes, I'm looking for a jacket for myself
예, 내가 입을 재킷을 찾고 있습니다.

S : How about this one? I think it'll look good on you.
이것은 어떻습니까? 손님에게 잘 어울릴 것 같은데요.

G : Yeah, I like it. Can I try it on?
예, 마음에 듭니다. 한 번 입어볼 수 있을까요?

S : Sure. The fitting room is over there.
물론이지요. 탈의실은 저쪽입니다.

Later 잠시 후

S : How does it fit?
잘 맞습니까?

G : (It's) too tight. May I have a larger one?
너무 꼭 끼입니다. 더 큰 것으로 주세요.

S : Here's half a size larger.
여기 반 인치 더 큰 것이 있습니다.

마음에 드는 옷을 입어보고 싶으면 Can I try this on?(한 번 입어볼 수 있을까요?)이라고 말하면 되고, 탈의실을 이용하고 싶으면 Where is your fitting room?(탈의실은 어디에 있습니까?)이라고 물어보면 된다. 옷이 사이즈별로 있는 경우에는 점원이 What size do you wear?(어떤 사이즈를 입으세요?)라고 물으면 자기가 평상시 입는 사이즈 I need a size 66.(사이즈 66을 주세요.)라고 대답하면 된다.

Dialogue *C*

S : May I help you? 무엇을 도와드릴까요?

G : Yes, What kind of stone is this? 예, 이것은 어떤 종류의 보석입니까?

S : It's a sapphire. We have only one broach of this type. Would you like to try it on? 그것은 사파이어입니다. 이런 모양의 브로치는 단 하나밖에 없습니다. 한 번 차 보시겠습니까?

G : Yes, I would. But how much is it? 예, 그러죠. 그런데 값이 얼마입니까?

S : Only one hundred and fifty dollars. 겨우 150달러입니다.

G : It's too expensive. It's over my budget. Do you have anything else within my budget?
너무 비싸고, 제 예산을 초과하는군요. 제 예산에 맞게 살 수 있는 것은 없습니까?

S : How about this one? This is just one hundred dollars and the same kind of stone as that one.
이것은 어떻습니까? 100달러인데, 저것과 같은 종류의 보석입니다.

G : I like it, but can you come down a little?
마음에 듭니다만, 조금 싸게 주시겠습니까?

S : Sorry, I can't. We go strictly by the price tag.
죄송합니다만, 저희는 정찰제를 철저히 지키고 있습니다.

어느 나라에서든지 물건을 구입할 때는 가격을 할인해서 사는 것이 현명한 쇼핑 방법일 것이다. 가격을 할인해 달라고 할 때 사람들이 No DC? DC, please.라고 말하는데 이것은 잘못된 표현으로 외국인들에게는 전혀 의미가 통하질 않는다. 올바른 표현은 Discount, please(할인 좀 해주세요) 또는 Can you come down a little?(좀 싸게 줄 수 없습니까?)라고 해야 한다. 원어민들은 절대로 discount를 DC라고 줄여 쓰지는 않는다.

Dialogue *D*

S : Sales women, G : Guest

S : Is there anything that interests you?
마음에 드는 물건이 있습니까?

G : Thank you. But I' m just looking around.
고맙습니다만 그냥 구경하는 거예요.

S : If you need any help, please let me know. My name is Jane.
만약에 도움이 필요하시면 말씀해 주세요. 제 이름은 제인입니다.

G : Thank you.
고맙습니다.

물건을 구입하지는 않지만, 외국의 백화점이나 쇼핑센터를 방문하여 구경을 하는 경우가 있다. 매장을 방문하면 점원들이 May I help you? 혹은 Is there anything that interests you?(마음에 드는 물건이 있습니까?)라고 물어보는데, 그냥 구경만 할 경우에는 I' m just looking around. 혹은 I' m just browsing through.(그냥 구경하는 거예요.)라고 말하면 된다. 물건을 구경만 하는 것을 우리나라에서는 eye shopping이라고 하는데 이것은 틀린 표현으로써 window shopping이라고 말해야 한다.

5 Role Play

Student A

A : 기념품을 찾고 계십니까?

B : Yes, I am. What kind of souvenirs do you have to take to Korea?

A : 대표적인 기념품으로 영국산 홍차, 우의, 도자기 등을 권해 드리고 싶군요.

B : Which of them do you recommend for me?

A : 기념품으로 많은 관광객들이 선호하는 것은 영국산 홍차입니다.

B : How much is this one?

A : 20불입니다.

B : Do you have a cheaper one?

A : 이것은 세트 당 15불입니다.

B : Oh, this seems good. I'll take it.

A : 좋습니다, 손님.

A : 이것은 어떤 종류의 보석입니까?

B : It's a sapphire. We have only one brooch of this type. Would you like to try it on?

A : 예, 그르지요. 그런데 값이 얼마입니까?

B : Only one hundred and fifty dollars.

A : 너무 비쌉니다. 저는 100달러를 가지고 있는데, 제 예산에 맞게 살 수 있는 것은 없습니까?

B : How about this one? This is just one hundred dollars and the same kind of stone as that one.

A : 좋습니다만, 디자인이 마음에 들지 않아요.

B : Ah, this is the last one that I recommend. It's coral, special from Hawaii. And the price is ninety dollars, which would be within your budget.

A : 좋습니다. 그것을 사겠습니다.

Student *B*

A : Are you looking for some souvenirs?

B : 예, 그렇습니다. 한국에 가지고 갈 좋은 기념품으로는 어떤 것이 있습니까?

A : For typical souvenirs, I recommend English tea, a rain coat, chinaware or something like that.

B : 그 중 어떤 물건이 좋겠습니까?

A : English tea is what many tourists take an interest in as souvenirs?

B : 이것은 값이 얼마입니까?

A : 20 dollars.

B : 더 싼 것은 없습니까?

A : This is $15 per set.

B : 이게 좋을 것 같네요. 이것을 사겠습니다.

A : All right, sir.

A : What kind of stone is this?

B : 그것은 사파이어입니다. 이런 모양의 브로치는 단 하나밖에 없습니다. 한 번 걸어 보시겠습니까?

A : Yes, I would. But how much is it?

B : 겨우 150달러입니다.

A : It's too expensive for me. My budget is one hundred dollars. Do you have anything else within my budget?

B : 이것은 어떻습니까? 꼭 100달러인데, 저것과 같은 종류의 보석입니다.

A : I like it, but I don't like the design.

B : 아, 그러면 마지막으로 하나 권해 드리겠습니다. 하와이의 특산물인 산호입니다. 90달러인데 당신의 예산에 맞으리라 생각됩니다.

A : O.K. I'll take it.

Unit 09

Shopping(Ⅱ)

1 Vocabulary and Patterns

* fitting room 탈의실
* try on 입어보다.

EX

A : May I try this on?
B : Sure. The fitting room is over there.

* look for ~을 찾다. / look good on ~에게 잘 어울리다.

EX

M : I'm looking for a sweater for myself. (TEPS L/C)
W : Sure. How about this one? I think it'll look good on you.
M : Yeah, I like it. Can I try it on?
W : ________________________ .

(a) Certainly. I like to try it on.
(b) No, I'm afraid we don't offer tailoring service.
(c) Sure. The fitting room is over there.
(d) Sure. You can try again.

* ring up (매상을) 금전등록기에 기록하다. 계산하다.

EX

A : Can you ring it up for me?
B : Certainly.

* copy=receipt 영수증

EX

A : Here's your copy.
B : Thank you.

* I'm just looking around. 그냥 구경하는 거예요.
(= I'm just browsing through.)
Would you show me this one? 이것 좀 보여주시겠어요?

유용한 표현들

쇼핑할 때 ...

① May I try this on?
한번 입어/신어/써 봐도 될까요?

② This is too tight.
나에게는 너무 작군요.

③ This is too loose.
나에게는 너무 크군요.

④ Do you have this in a smaller size?
이걸로 좀 더 작은 것은 없습니까?

⑤ Do you have this in a different color?
이걸로 다른 색깔은 없습니까?

⑥ Could you show me this?
(진열장 안에 있는 것을 보고) 이것 좀 볼 수 있을까요?

⑦ I think I'll look around a little bit.
다른데도 좀 보고 다시 오겠습니다.

⑧ Could you gift-wrap this?
이것을 선물용으로 포장해 주시겠습니까?

⑨ Where can I find the computer?
컴퓨터 파는 곳은 어디입니까?

⑩ I think it's too much. Could you sell it for $ 5?
값이 너무 비싼 것 같아요. 5달라에 판매하세요.

⑪ Would you take $10 for two?
두 개에 10달러에 주시겠어요?

2 Utterance-Response Drills

Can I help you?

I' m going for a lightweight jacket.

Would you care to look at these?

I need something I can pack easily. I' ll be traveling a lot.

These are especially good for traveling. They don' t wrinkle. Try one on.

Hmm... not bad. I think I' ll get this one.

May I try it on?

Of course. There is the fitting room over there.

How do you like it?

It fits, but the sleeves are too long.

No problem. We can shorten them for you.

OK. I' ll take it.

Will this be cash or charge?

Will you take my traveller' s check?

Well, I' m looking for a gift and I want to stay under twenty dollars.

I see. Is this gift for a man or a woman?

A woman.

Did you have anything special in mind?

Not really. I don' t know what to get her.

Hello! May I help you?

No, thank you. I' m just looking.

OK. Let me know if there is anything that I can help you with.

Thank you. I will.

3 Role Play

Student 𝔄

A : 구두를 한 켤레 사고 싶은데요.

B : For yourself, sir?

A : 예.

B : What's your size?

A : 160cm입니다.

B : I think One hundred sixty centimeters is equivalent to size six. What kind of style do you have in mind?

A : 이런 모양이 좋군요. 어떤 색깔이 있죠?

B : Black, brown, dark brown, and white.

A : 짙은 갈색 구두를 보여주세요.

B : Yes, sir. Will you try them on?

A : 예, 그러죠.

B : How do you feel? They are made in France and in fashion here.

A : 흐음!... 발이 아주 편하군요. 가격은 얼마죠?

B : Fifty dollars.

A : 이거 얼마죠?

B : Six hundred dollars.

A : 좀 비싸군요. 깎아 주시면 살 수 있지만.

B : Well, $ 400.

A : 150달러로 하지요.

B : No no, that's absurd. $ 300 is the best I can do.

A : 좋아요. 알았어요. 그럼 200달러 어때요?

B : But, I won't make a profit. $ 250, I can't do better than that.

A : 좋습니다. 250달러 내지요.

B : OK. I guess so. You are certainly good at bargaining!

Student B

A : I want to but a pair of shoes.

B : 손님이 신으실 겁니까?

A : Yes.

B : 사이즈가 어떻게 됩니까?

A : One hundred sixty centimeters.

B : 160cm라면 사이즈 6에 해당될 것 같군요. 어떤 스타일을 생각하고 계십니까?

A : I like this style. What kind of color do you have?

B : 검은 색, 갈색, 짙은 갈색, 그리고 흰색이 있습니다.

A : Show me the dark brown ones, please.

B : 알겠습니다, 손님. 신어 보시겠습니까?

A : OK. I will.

B : 맞습니까? 그 구두는 프랑스제인데, 이곳에서 유행하고 있습니다.

A : Hm!... They are very comfortable. How much?

B : 50달러입니다.

A : How much does this cost?

B : 600달러인데요.

A : It's a little expensive. If you make it a little cheaper, I might buy it.

B : 그럼 400달러로 합시다.

A : $ 150.

B : 안돼요. 그럴 순 없어요. 300달러면 최대한으로 싸게 드리는 겁니다.

A : OK, I understand. Well, how about $ 200?

B : 그럼, 제가 남는 게 없다고요. 250달러 이하로는 깎아줄 수가 없어요.

A : OK, I'll pay $ 250.

B : 그래요. 물건 사는 솜씨가 보통이 아니군요.

Unit 10

Telephone(I)

1 Vocabulary and Patterns

1. 상대를 확인하는 표현

Hello, is that the Accounts Department? 여보세요, 거기 경리부인가요?

Is Joe Johnson in? 조 쟌슨씨 계신가요?

Is Prof. Bae there? 배 교수님 계신가요?

Is that 842-2924?

2. ~좀 바꿔 주세요.

May I Could I Can I I'd like to	speak to Miss Kim, please? speak to the Manager, please? have the Accounts Department, please?

※ 응답자가 전화를 걸어온 쪽에서 통화하고자 하는 사람인 경우엔 "This is he/she (speaking)." 혹은 "Speaking."이라고 답한다.

※ 한참 통화하다가 "누구를 바꿔주세요"라고 할 때는 "Put 누구 on, please."라고 말한다.

3. 전화거시는 분은 누구죠?

Who's calling, please?

Who's speaking, please?

Can I have your name, please?

May I ask who's calling?

※ Who shall I say is calling? 어느 분께서 전화주셨다고 할까요?
비서나 교환이 주로 쓰는 표현

※ Who am I speaking to? 전화 받으시는 분은 누구세요?

※ 응답 표현

This is James Bond, from Hilton Hotel.
저는 힐튼호텔의 제임스 본드입니다.

This is Mr. Kelly's secretary.
저는 켈리씨의 비서예요.

Jae-il Machinery.
제일 기계입니다.

I'm calling on behalf of Mr. Song.
송선생을 대신해서 전화 드리는 건데요.

4. 잠깐만 기다려주세요

Hold the line, please.

Hold on, please.

One moment, please.

Just a moment, please.

5. 상태가 안 좋은데...

I'm sorry I'm afraid it's a bad line.	I can't hear you. we have a bad connection.

위의 말을 마친 후.

Can you speak a little louder?
Can you hang up and call back?
Hang up and I'll call you back.

※ I'll get him/her for you. = He/She will be right with you.
곧 바꿔드리겠습니다.

6. 전화를 잘못 거신 것 같군요.

I'm sorry I'm afraid	you've got the wrong number. there's no one of that name here. the number's been changed. you have the wrong extension. Hold the line and I'll try to transfer you.

7. 미안합니다. 제가 전화를 잘못 걸었군요.

I'm (terribly) sorry Sorry to bother you Excuse me	I've got the wrong number. I must have the wrong number. I must have dialed the wrong number.

※ 상대방으로부터 사과의 말을 들었을 경우에는 아무 말없이 전화를 끊기보다는

That's O. K.	That's all right.
Don't mention it.	No problem.

이란 말을 해주는 것이 예의.

2 Patterns Drill

(1) May I speak to Mr. Brown?

Can talk

I'd like to

(2) May I ask who's calling?

know talking

speaking

(3) You have the wrong number.

You've got

I'm afraid you've dialed

(4) Hold the line, please.

Wait a minute

Just a moment

Hold on

3 Role Play

Student A

A : 네, 총무과입니다.

B : Good morning. May I speak to Mr. Park, please?

A : 전화거시는 분은 누구신가요?

B : This is James Nolan.

A : 잠깐만 기다려 주세요. 그분은 내선 107번인데, 연결시켜드리죠.

A : 여보세요, 영업부입니다.

B : May I speak to Miss Jeong, please?

A : 미스 정이요? 아, 이쪽이 아니고요. 미스 정은 내선 286번입니다. 잠깐 기다리세요. 제가 그 쪽으로 돌려 드릴게요.

B : Thank you.

A : 여보세요.

B : Hello. May I speak to Mr. Kim?

A : 그런 이름 가지신 분은 여기 없는데요. 전화를 잘못 걸으셨군요.

B : What number is that?

A : 45-5282인데요.

B : Oh, I'm sorry. I must have dialed the wrong number.

A : 괜찮습니다.

A : 네. 한진 여행사입니다. 도와드릴까요?

B : Is Miss. Bae there?

A : 죄송하지만, 소리가 잘 안 들리는데. 좀 큰 소리로 말씀해 주시겠습니까?

B : Can I speak to Miss Bae, please?

A : 연결 상태가 좋지 않군요. 끊고 다시 걸어주시죠.

B : Yes, I'll call back.

Student B

A : Good morning, General Affairs Department.

B : 안녕하세요. 미스터 박 좀 부탁합니다.

A : Who's calling, please?

B : 전 제임스 놀란입니다.

A : Hold on, please. He's on extension 107. I'll put you through to him.

A : Hello. Sales Department.

B : 미스 정 좀 바꿔 주시겠습니까?

A : Miss Jeong? Oh, you have the wrong extension. She's on extension 268. Hold the line, and I'll transfer you.

B : 감사합니다.

A : Hello.

B : 여보세요. 미스터 김 좀 바꿔 주십시오.

A : There's no one of that name here. You must have the wrong number.

B : 몇 번이죠?

A : This is 45-5282.

B : 아, 죄송합니다. 전화를 잘못 걸었군요.

A : No problem.

A : Hello. Hanjin Travel Agency Co., Ltd. May I help you?

B : 미스 배 있습니까?

A : I'm sorry, I can't hear you. Can you speak a bit louder?

B : 미스 배 좀 바꿔 주세요.

A : We have a bad line. Could you hang up and call back?

B : 예, 다시 전화 걸죠.

Unit 11 Telephone(Ⅱ)

1 Vocabulary and Patterns

1. 그 분은 지금 바쁘십니다.

I'm sorry I'm afraid	he's she's	busy./tied up./occupied. on the line. on another line. in conference. with a client.

Caller가 원하는 상대가 다른 용무로 인해 전화를 받을 수 없을 경우에 답하는 요령이다. 「그래도 기다리겠냐」는 뜻으로

Would you care to hold or could I take a message?
Do you want to hold?
Would you mind holding?

이라는 말을 덧붙인다면 전화응답으로는 수준급.

2. 그 분은 지금 자리에 없습니다.

I'm sorry I'm sorry Sorry but	he's she's	out. not in the office. just gone[stepped] out. not available now. away on business. on a business trip. out of town.

3. 언제 들어올지 아세요?

Oh, when will he be back?
When do you expect him back?
When is she expected?
Can you tell me when he'll be back?
Do you know when she'll be in?

4. 그럼, 언제쯤 통화할 수 있겠습니까?

Oh, I see Could you tell me when she'll be available?
When will he be free?
Have you any idea when he'll be free?
What time do you think he'll be free?
Do you know when he'll be finished?

5. 메모를 남기시겠어요?

Can/ Could/ May I take a message?
Would you like to leave a message?
Is there any message?
If you like, I can take a message.

만약 전화를 건 사람의 입장에서 「메모를 남기고 싶다」고 말할 경우엔 Can/Could/May I leave a message?라고 말하면 된다.
전달 사항을 남기고 싶을 때는 Thanks, please tell her that ~. Yes, please let him know that ~. 등의 패턴을 이용한다.

6. 아닙니다. 제가 나중에 다시 전화 드리죠.

No, thanks.

No, thank you.

That's okay. I'll call back later.

It's not urgent.

I'll try later.

7. ~로 전화해 달라고 전해 주세요.

This is 이름 and number's 번호.

Please tell him to call me.

Could you ask him to call 이름 + 번호.

Please have him call 이름 at 번호.

2 Role Play

Student A

A : 여보세요. 한일 회사입니다.

B : Good morning. Can I speak to Mr. Adams, please?

A : 죄송합니다만, 지금 출장 중이신데요.

B : Oh, when will he be back?

A : 5월 15일 돌아오실 겁니다. 다른 분이라도 바꿔 드릴까요?

B : No, thank you. I'll call back later.

A : 여보세요. 한선생 좀 바꿔 주세요.

B : Who's calling, please?

A : 미스터 씨튼입니다.

B : Hold the line please, Mr. Seaton... Hello, I'm afraid Mr. Han's in conference at the moment.

A : 오, 알겠습니다. 언제쯤 통화할 수 있겠습니까?

B : He should be free at 4 o'clock.

A : 예, 오늘 오후에 제게 전화해달라고 전해주세요.

B : Certainly. Can I have your name and number, please?

A : 이름은...시튼, 그리고 번호는 765-4434입니다.

B : Can you spell your name, please?

A : 예. 에스-이-에이-티-오-앤입니다.

B : Thank you, Mr. Seaton. I'll give Mr. Han the message.

A : 감사합니다. 그럼...

B : Good-bye.

Student *B*

A : Good morning. Hanil Company.

B : 네, 애덤즈 씨 좀 바꿔 주시죠?

A : I'm sorry, he's away on business at present.

B : 아, 언제 돌아오십니까?

A : He should be back on 15th May. Can anybody else help you?

B : 아닙니다. 나중에 다시 전화 드리죠.

A : Hello. Can I speak to Mr. Han, please?

B : 누구신가요?

A : This is Mr. Seaton.

B : 잠시만 기다려 주십시오, 씨튼氏... 여보세요. 죄송합니다만 한선생은 지금 회의 중이신데요.

A : Oh, I see. When will he be free?

B : 4시엔 시간이 나실 겁니다. 메모를 남기시겠어요?

A : Yes. Would you ask him to call me back this afternoon?

B : 그르죠. 성함과 연락처를 말씀해 주세요.

A : Yes. S-E-A-T-O-N.

B : 감사합니다, 시튼氏. 한 선생께 전해드리죠.

A : Thank you, bye.

B : 안녕히 계십시오.

Unit 12 Telephone(Ⅲ)

1 Vocabulary and Patterns

1. Person to Person Call(지명통화)(지배인면접)

국제전화에서는 자가 통화하고 싶은 상대방을 지명하는 것이 가능하다. 이 경우 지명료가 가산되지만 지명된 사람이 전화기에 나올 때까지 요금은 계산되지 않는다. 상대방이 없을 때는 요금을 내지 않는다.

> I'd like to make a person-to-person call to Thomas Edison at area code 318, 455-7201.
> 지역번호는 318, 455국의 7201번의 토마스 에디슨에게 지명통화를 하고 싶습니다.

2. Credit Card Call(크레디트 카드 콜)

국제 전신전화국에서 발행한 Credit Card를 이용하여 통화하는 방법이다. 요금은 Credit Card의 계약시 지정한 회사, 혹은 개인에게 청구되어진다.

3. Station to Station Call(전화번호 지정 통화)

4. Collect Call(수신인 부담 통화)

통화 요금을 상대방에게 부담시키는 방식이다. 따라서 교환은 수신자가 통화 요금을 지불할 의사가 있는가를 문의한 후 전화를 연결해 준다.

I'd like to make a collect call to Solomon at area code 852, 806-9966. My name is Sang-jeong, Bae.
솔로몬에게 수신인 지불통화를 하고 싶은데, 지역번호는 852, 806국의 9966번입니다. 제 이름은 배상정입니다.

I'd like to call Lois Banks at area code 406, 544-3322, and please reverse the charges(또는 make it a collect call). My name is Young-il, Kim.
로이스 뱅크스에게 통화하려는데요, 지역번호는 406, 544의 3322번입니다. 요금은 수신자 부담으로 하세요. 제 이름은 김영일입니다.

5. Overseas call(국제 전화)

I'd like to make an overseas call to Seoul, Korea, the number is 967-4321.
대한민국 서울로 국제전화를 하고 싶은데요. 번호는 967의 4321번입니다.

국제전화에는 이상과 같은 종류가 있기 때문에 시간, 장소에 따라 적절한 통화 방법을 선택하는 것이 바람직하다. 예를 들어 특정인과의 통화가 아니라 단순히 집안에 안부를 알리는 일이라면 Station-to-Station Call, 특별히 통화하고 싶은 사람이 있을 때는 Person-to-Person Call, 여행 중 여비를 아끼고 싶거나 전화에 필요한 잔돈이 없을 때에는 Collect Call, 또 사업 등 자주 전화를 이용하는 사람에게는 Credit Card Call이 편리할 것이다.

Asking for information

Could you give me information on ~ ?
~에 대해서 정보를 좀 주시겠습니까?

I wonder if you could tell me about ~
~에 대해서 말씀해 주실 수 있을지 모르겠군요.

I'd appreciate it if you could give some information about ~
~에 대해서 알려 주시면 고맙겠습니다.

I' m phoning to inquire about ~
~에 대해서 문의하려고 전화 드렸습니다.

I' d like to talk to inquire about ~
~에 대해서 아시는 분과 통화 좀 했으면 싶군요.

문의에 응하기

① 바로 답할 수 있을 때

Just a moment, I' ll get you that information.
잠시만요, 그 정보를 알려 드리겠습니다.

Could you hold the line, I' ll back.
잠깐만 기다려 주실래요, 알아보겠습니다.

Please hold a second, I' ll see.
잠깐만요, 알아봐 드리죠.

Hold on a moment, please.
잠시만 기다려 주세요.

② 시간이 좀 필요할 때

Could I call you back on that in a few minutes?

Would you mind if I got back to you on that in a few minutes?

How about if I call you back in a few minutes?
몇 분 후에 제가 전화를 다시 걸어 알려드리면 안 될까요?

Would you like to hold or should I call you back after I' ve checked?
기다리겠습니까 아니면 제가 알아보고 다시 전화 드릴까요?

다른 곳을 추천

I'm sorry, we don't have that information. I suggest you call ~ .
유감스럽게도 저흰 그런 정보가 없습니다. ~로 전화해 보시죠.

I'm afraid you have the wrong department. Maybe you should try ~ .
부서가 잘못 연결된 것 같군요. 아마 ~로 연락해 보세요.

Let me connect you with Mr. Kim, who may have the answer.
미스터 김을 연결시켜 드리겠습니다. 그분은 알고 계실 겁니다.

In that case, the person you want is Mr. Choi.
그런 경우라면, 최선생하고 얘기하셔야 합니다.

Miss Park may be able to help you.
미스 박이 도와드릴 수 있을 겁니다.

2 Role Play

Student A

A : 장거리 전화를 부탁합니다.

B : Is this person-to-person or collect?

A : 컬렉트콜로 하겠습니다. 번호는 722-9748입니다.

B : Please wait.

A : 국제전화 교환입니다. 무엇을 도와 드릴까요?

B : Yes, I want to make an international call to Seoul, Korea. And make it collect, please.

A : 서울 전화는 몇 번인가요?

B : The area code 02, and the number is 234-1234.

A : 댁의 번호는요?

B : My number is (212)432-1234, and name is Song, S.O.N.G.

A : 교환입니다.

B : I want to make a person-to-person call to 212-836-1725.

A : 통화하실 분의 성함은요?

B : Ed Cooper. That's C, double-O, P, E, R.

A : 알겠습니다. 기다리세요. 연결해 드리겠습니다.

B : Thank you.

A : 탐 브라운으로부터의 컬렉트콜을 받겠습니까?

B : Yes, I will accept.

A : 전화 끊지 말고 기다릴까요, 그쪽에서 걸어주시겠어요?

B : Hold the line... Here's your party now.

Student *B*

A : I'd like to make a long distance call.

B : 지명통화인가요, 아니면 컬렉트콜인가요?

A : Collect. The number is 722-9784.

B : 잠깐만 기다리세요.

A : International operator. May I help you?

B : 네, 서울에 국제전화를 걸고 싶은데요. 그리고 컬렉트콜로 해주십시오.

A : What's the number in Seoul.

B : 지역번호는 02, 그리고 전화번호는 234-1234입니다.

A : Your number and name, please?

B : 제 번호는 212-432-4321입니다. 그리고 이름은 송이구요.

A : Operator.

B : 212-836-1725로 지명 통화를 하고 싶은데요.

A : What's the name of the party you're calling?

B : 에드 쿠퍼입니다. C와 O 두 개와 P, E, R입니다.

A : Okay. Please wait while I put you through.

B : 고맙습니다.

A : Will you accept a collect call from Tom Brown?

B : 예, 받겠습니다.

A : Shall I hold the line or will you call me back?

B : 기다리세요. 상대편이 나옵니다. 어서 말씀하세요.

Unit 13 At the Restaurant

1 Vocabulary and Patterns

1) 요리 방법을 묻는 표현과 대답

How would you like (to have) your How do you want your	meat? steak? eggs?

① 스테이크를 굽는데는 보통 3가지가 있다.

well done	아주 바싹 구운 것
medium	알맞게 구운 것
rare	약간 안 익게 구운 것

② 계란의 요리법은 보통 다음과 같은 종류가 있다.

soft-boiled	반숙한 것
hard-boiled	완숙한 것
sunny-side up	한쪽만 프라이한 것
(tipped) over	양쪽 다 프라이한 것
scrambled	버터와 달걀을 섞어서 부쳐낸 것

2) 음식의 주문과 대답

What would you like to have? 무엇을 드시겠습니까?

I'd like I'll have	음식이름
음식이름	will be fine. , please.

I'll have New York steak.

I'd like T-bone steak.

Lobster, please.

Tenderloin steak will be fine.

3) 접객 및 자리 안내

Hello. How many (in your party)? 어서 오십시오. 몇 분이십니까?

May I ask the name the reservation was made under?
예약하신 분의 성함이 어떻게 되십니까?

Do you have a table available? 지금 빈자리가 있습니까?

I'm sorry. We don't have a table available right now.
죄송합니다만, 지금 빈자리가 없습니다.

4) 식사 및 요리 주문

Can I have a menu, please. 메뉴판 좀 갖다 주세요.

What is the special menu of the day? 오늘의 특별 메뉴는 무엇입니까?

What is the most popular dish in this restaurant?
이 레스토랑에서 가장 인기 있는 메뉴는 무엇입니까?

What is the name of this dish? 이 요리의 이름은 무엇입니까?

What is this made of? 이것은 무슨 재료로 만드나요?

Is this spicy? 이것은 맵습니까?

May I change my order? 주문을 바꿔도 되겠습니까?

This steak is overcooked. 이 스테이크는 너무 익혔는데요.

It's salty/ bland / spicy. 음식이 너무 짭니다. 싱거워요/매워요.

5) 칵테일 바에서

칵테일 바에서 '무엇을 드릴까요?' 라는 표현은 'What will it be?' 이며 같은 표현으로 'What's your pleasure?' 를 쓰기도 한다. 스카치 위스키에 '얼음을 넣어 드릴까요?' 라는 표현은 'On the rocks?' 라고 표현하며 얼음을 넣지 않고 그냥 마실 때는 'straight' 라고 표현한다.

6) 음식명 영어표기(한국관광공사. 2009)

■ 양식

우리말	영어표기	우리말	영어표기
오므라이스	omelette rice	카레라이스	curried rice
돈가스	pork cutlet	비후가스	beef cutlet
등심스테이크	sirloin steak	안심스테이크	beef tenderloin steak
티본스테이크	T-bone steak	함박스테이크	hamburger steak
고기햄버거	meat hamburger	야채 버거	vegetable burger
야채햄버거	vegetable hamburger	치즈버거	cheese burger
감자튀김	french fries / chips	피자	pizza
콤비네이션피자	combination pizza	해물피자	seafood pizza
야채수프	vegetable soup	크림수프	cream soup
미트스파게티	meat spaghetti	스파게티	spaghetti
야채샐러드	vegetable salad	훈제연어	smoked salmon

■ 한식

우리말	영어표기
불고기 백반	set meal with bulgogi
간장게장백반	set meal with marinated crab
된장찌개백반	set meal with soybean paste stew
순두부백반	set meal with soft tofu
꼬치(오뎅)백반	rice with fish sausage
백반 정식	set meal with rice and side dishes
수육	boiled beef cold cuts
갈비찜	braised beef ribs
아귀찜	steamed angler fish
소머리국밥	ox head soup with rice
보리밥	barley rice
돌솥비빔밥	bibimbap in a hot stone pot
비빔밥	bibimbap (cooked rice served with vegetables and sometimes meat to mix in the bowl at the table)
산채비빔밥	bibimbap with wild vegetables
열무비빔밥	bibimbap with young radishes
물냉면	buckwheat noodles in chilled broth
비빔냉면	cold buckwheat noodles with red hot peeper paste
오징어볶음	stir-fried cuttlefish with vegetables
갈비구이	marinated and grilled beef ribs
삼치구이	broiled spanish mackerel
생선구이	grilled fish
갈치구이	grilled hairtail fish
곱창구이	grilled beef tripe
오리구이	grilled duck
김치볶음밥	stir-fried rice with kimchi
양송이볶음밥	stir-fried rich with mushrooms
오징어볶음밥	stir-fried rich with cuttlefish
LA갈비	marinated beef ribs

우리말	영어표기
닭갈비	pan-fried chicken
돼지갈비	grilled pork rips
불 갈비	grilled beef ribs
소갈비	beef ribs
만둣국	dumpling soup
미역국	seaweed soup
선지국	ox blood soup
우거짓국	chinese cabbage soup
콩나물국	soy-bean sprout soup
해장국	soup for hangovers
갈비탕	beef rib soup
감자탕	pork rip soup with potatoes
곰탕	boiled beef soup
꼬리곰탕	ox-tail stew
꽃게탕	blue crab stew
대구탕	codfish soup
도가니탕	ox-knee soup
복매운탕	spicy puffer fish stew
사골 우거지탕	beef and vegetable stew
삼계탕	chicken ginseng soup
백숙	stuffed chicken stew
생선매운탕	spicy fish stew
설렁탕	ox bone soup
쏘가리매운탕	spicy mandarin fish stew
아구탕	spicy angler fish stew
오골계탕	ogol chicken stew
우거지갈비탕	beef rib stew with vegetables
추어탕	loach soup
해물매운탕	spicy seafood stew
구절판	platter of nine delicacies

우리말	영어표기
불고기	bulgogi
삼겹살	grilled pork loin
생등심	beef sirloin
신선로	court-style casserole
육개장	spicy beef and leek soup
육회	sliced raw beef
청국장	thick soybean paste soup
곱창전골	spicy beef tripe casserole
국수전골	noodle casserole
궁중전골	court-style casserole
김치전골	kimchi casserole
낙지전골	baby octopus casserole
모듬전골	assorted beef and vegetables casserole
버섯전골	mushroom casserole
소고기전골	beef soup (casserole)
해물전골	seafood casserole
김치찌개	kimchi stew
동태찌개	pollack stew
된장찌개	soybean paste stew
순두부찌개	spicy soft tofu stew
볶음밥	stir-fried rice

■ 일식

우리말	영어표기
덴동정식	Japanese deep-fry mix set
튀김정식	set meal with deep fry
생신조림	braised fish
김초밥	laver sushi
생선초밥	sushi

우리말	영어표기
유부초밥	fried tofu rice roll
송이덮밥	rice topped with pine mushrooms
장어덮밥	rice topped with broiled eel
회덮밥	rice topped with raw fish
복탕	spicy puffer fish stew
알탕	spicy fish roe stew
우럭탕	rock fish stew
계란찜	steamed egg
멍게	sea squirt
메밀국수	buckwheat noodles
샤브샤브	shabu-shabu
전복죽	rice porridge with abalone
해삼	sea cucumber
꽁치구이	grilled mackerel
도미구이	grilled sea bream
삼치구이	broiled Spanish mackerel
생선구이	grilled fish
장어구이	grilled Eel
철판구이	grill on a hot metal plate
대구탕	codfish soup
숭어회	raw gray mullet
꽃게탕	blue crab stew
내장탕	beef tripe and intestine soup
대합탕	clam stew
도미탕	sea bream stew
아구탕	spicy angler fish stew
조개탕	spicy hot clam soup

■ 중식

우리말	영어표기
기스면	noodle soup with chicken broth
간 자장	noodles with black soybean sauce
삼선 간 자장	seafood noodles with black soybean sauce
삼선자장	seafood noodles with black soybean sauce
자장면	noodles with black soybean sauce
삼선우동(가락국수)	seafood udon
우동	udong
울면	noodles in thickened broth
짬뽕	spicy noodle soup
삼선볶음밥	stir-fried rice with seafood
새우볶음밥	stir-fried rice with shrimps
송이덮밥	rice topped with pine mushrooms
자장밥	rice topped with black soybean sauce
잡탕밥	rice with assorted seafood
잡채밥	stir-fried potato noodles with vegetables and rice
군만두	fried dumplings
물만두	boiled dumplings
군만두(야끼만두)	fried dumplings
깐풍기	fried chicken with hot pepper sauce
라조기	stir-fried chicken with hot sauce
라조육	stir-fried fish with hot sauce
소고기튀김	deep-fried beef
새우튀김	deep-fried shrimps
튀김	deep-fried vegetables and fish
탕수육	sweet and sour pork
팔보채	stir-fried seafood and vegetables
해삼탕	sea cucumber soup

■ 분식

우리말	영어표기
바지락 칼국수	hand-rolled noodle soup with clams
막국수	buckwheat noodles with vegetables
메밀국수	buckwheat noodles
비빔국수	noodles with vegetables and red hot peeper paste
손칼국수	hand-rolled noodle soup
칼국수	hand-rolled noodle soup
콩국수	chilled white bean soup noodles
떡볶이	rice cake and vegetables simmered in red hot peeper paste
라면	ramen
냉면	cold buckwheat noodles
비빔냉면	cold buckwheat noodles with red hot peeper paste
쫄면	chewy cold noodles
김밥	laver rice rolls
떡국	rice cake soup
수제비	dough flakes soup
순대	Korean black pudding
오징어튀김	deep-fried cuttlefish
김치만두	kimchi dumplings
고기만두	meat dumplings
만두	dumplings
군만두	fried dumplings
찐만두	steamed dumplings
떡만두국	rice cake soup with dumplings
만둣국	dumpling soup

■ 기타

우리말	영어표기
골뱅이무침	spicy freshwater snails
과일	fruits
김치전	kimchi pancake
두부김치	tofu and kimchi
마른안주	dry snacks
닭 강정	deep-fried sugar glazed chicken
전기구이통닭	grilled chicken
파전	green onion pancake

7) 한국 전통 식품의 영어표기(농수산부)

김치류	Kimchi로 표기 통일
깍두기김치	Kimchi(Radish roots kimchi)
나박김치	Kimchi(Watery kimchi)
동치미김치	Kimchi(Watery radish kimchi)
배추김치	Kimchi(Cabbage kimchi)
무청김치	Kimchi(Radish leaf kimchi)
유채김치	Kimchi(Rape leaf kimchi)
갓잎김치	Kimchi(Mustard leaf kimchi)
갓줄기김치	Kimchi(Mustard stem kimchi)

장류	외국의 hot sauce, chilli sauce와 구별 표기
고추장	Korean hot pepper paste(Gochujang)
간장	Soy sauce
된장	Soybean paste(Doenjang)
청국장	Soybean paste(Chonggugjang)

죽	(분말죽류 : soup powder, 죽 : 물이 포함된 것 soup)
호박죽	Pumpkin soup powder
들깨죽	Perilla soup powder
쌀죽	Rice soup powder
현미죽	Brown rice soup powder
찹쌀죽	Sweet rice soup powder
율무죽	Job's tears soup powder
단팥죽	Red bean soup powder

국수	Noodle로 표기 통일하고 메밀냉면만 vermicelli로 구별 표기
즉석면(라면)	Instant noodles
쑥국수	Mugwort noodles
칡국수	Arrowroot noodles
도토리국수	Acorn noodles
메밀국수	Buckwheat noodles
쌀국수	Rice noodles
감자국수	Potato noodles
메밀냉면	Buckwheat vermicelli

묵류	curd로 통일 표기
메밀묵	Buckwheat curd
도토리묵	Acorn curd

미숫가루	Parched + 품목명 + powder로 통일 표기
쌀미숫가루	Parched rice powder
찹쌀미숫가루	Parched sweet rice powder
보리미숫가루	Parched barley powder
쌀보리미숫가루	Parched naked barley powder
수수미숫가루	Parched sorghum powder
조미숫가루	Parched millet powder

건채류	Dried + 품목명 + slice로 통일 표기
무말랭이	Dried radish slice
호박고지	Dried squash/pumpkin slice
가지말랭이	Dried eggplant slice
박고지	Dried guard slice
토란말랭이	Dried taro stem slice
도라지말랭이	Dried bell-flower root slice
산채나물	Edible greens
실고추	Shredded red pepper

절임	품목 + pickle로 통일 표기
단무지	Radish pickle
오이지	Cucumber pickle
염교	Scallion pickle
달래지	Wild garlic pickle
깻잎지	Perilla leaf pickle

음료	nectar로 표기(수정과는 건물이 포함되지 않으므로 punch로 표기
식혜	Rice nectar
수정과	Sweet cinnamon punch
소주	Soju
약주	Rice wine(clear)
탁주	Rice wine(cloudy)

차류	품목명 + tea로 통일 표기
계피차	Cinnamon tea
구기자차	Boxthron tea
치커리차	Chicory tea
컴프리차	Comfry tea
유자차	Citron tea
인삼차	Korean ginseng tea

녹차	Green tea
감잎차	Persimmon leaf tea
홍차	Black tea
옥수수차	Corn tea

해조류	fried + 품목명으로 통일 표기
말린김	Dried laver
조미김	Seasoned, roasted laver
돌김	Natural laver
미역	Sea mustard
염장미역	Salted sea mustard
미역튀각	Fried sea mustard
다시마튀각	Fried sea tangle
건파래	Dried sea lettuce
말린다시마	Dried sea tangle
다시마말이	Rolled sea tangle

젓갈류	젓갈류에는 fermented란 표기없이 Salted+품목명으로 통일 표기(액젓의 경우 품목명 + sauce로 통일 표기)
새우젓	Salted shrimp
멸치젓	Salted anchovy
명란젓	Salted pollack egg
창란젓	Salted viscera
밴댕이젓	Salted shad
황새기젓	Salted sword fish
굴젓	Salted oyster
전복젓	Salted abalone
조개젓	Salted clam
게젓	Salted crab
멸치액젓	Anchovy sauce

한과류	Korean cracker( ) 안에 품목명 영어로 표기
강정	Korean cracker(Gangjung)
유과	Korean cracker(Yoogwa)
약과	Korean cracker(Yakgwa)
전병	Korean cracker(Junbyung)
산자	Korean cracker(Shanja)

만두류	Dumpling으로 표기하되 내용물의 영어명을 그 앞에 표기
야채만두	Vegetable dumpling
쇠고기만두	Beef dumpling
돼지고기만두	Pork dumpling
꿩만두	Pheasant dumpling
김치만두	Kimchi dumpling

기 타	
감식초	Persimmon vinegar
죽염	Salt roasted in bamboo
물엿	Dextrose syrup
삼계탕	Chicken stew with ginseng
엿기름	Malt
누룽지	Nurungji(Roasted cooking rice)

2 Patterns Drill

(1) What did you have for breakfast?
lunch
dinner
brunch

(2) What kind of food would you like to have?
drink
wine
salad

(3) How would you like to have your steak?
eggs
meat

(4) I always enjoy (a cup of) coffee after work.
milk
wine
lemonade

3 Utterance-Response Drills

Hello, welcome to Arby's.

Hi. I'll have a roast beef sandwich and a small fries.

Would you like a soda with that?

I think I will have a chocolate milk shake.

Hi. Welcome to Burger Chef. Can I take your order?

Yes, I will have a bacon cheeseburger.

Something to drink with that?

Step over to the right to get your order. You get your soda over there at the machine.

Hi. I just want a salad bar.

Okay. Here's your plate.

Do I come back here for a new plate if I want seconds?

Yes. That will be $2.95.

Here's three.

Five cents is your change. Thanks.

I'll have a chicken sandwich.

Is that for here or to go?

It will be to go, please.

Here you go.

Excuse me, this is not what I ordered. I ordered the chicken special.

I'm sorry, I must have misunderstood your order. I'll get the chicken special right away.

Thanks.

4 Dialogue

Dialogue A

W : Waiter, G : Guest

W : Good morning. May I take your order?
안녕하십니까, 주문하시겠습니까?

G : Yes, I'd like to have the Continental breakfast.
예, 저는 유럽식 조식으로 식사하고 싶습니다.

W : Would you like to have orange juice or milk?
오렌지 주스로 드시겠습니까? 우유로 드시겠습니까?

G : Orange juice, please.
오렌지 주스로 주세요.

W : Would you like coffee or tea?
커피를 드시겠습니까? 홍차를 드시겠습니까?

G : Coffee, please.
커피로 주세요.

W : Cream and sugar is on the table.
크림과 설탕은 테이블 위에 있습니다.

G : Thank you.
감사합니다.

호텔에서 숙박을 한 후 호텔 식당에서 조식을 먹는 경우가 많다. 스테이크를 주문해서 먹는 경우도 있지만 대부분 Continental breakfast나 American Breakfast를 주문하는 경우가 많다. Continental breakfast는 빵과 주스나 우유가 제공되는 간단한 유럽식 조식이다. 패키지 여행의 경우 미주나 유럽쪽 호텔에선 Continental breakfast가 제공되고, 아시아쪽 호텔에선 American Breakfast(미국식 조식)나 Buffet(뷔페)가 제공된다. 음료수는 주스나 우유 중에서 선택하면 되고 커피는 식사 전에 무제한으로 제공되는 곳도 많다.

Dialogue 𝓑

W : Waiter, G : Guest

W : Are you ready to order now? 지금 주문하시겠습니까?

G : Yes. 예

W : What would you like to have? 무엇을 드시겠습니까?

G : I' ll have a New York Steak. 뉴욕 스테이크로 하겠습니다.

W : How would you like it(that done)? 어떻게 익혀드릴까요?

G : Well done, please. 잘 익혀 주세요.

W : Baked potatoes or rice? 구운 감자로 하시겠습니까, 밥으로 하시겠습니까?

G : Baked potato, please. 구운 감자로 주세요.

W : Soup or salad? 수프를 드시겠습니까, 샐러드로 드시겠습니까?

G : Salad. please. 샐러드로 주세요.

W : What kind of dressing would you like? 드레싱은 뭐로 할까요?

G : (I' d like) Thousand Island. 따우전 아일랜드로 주세요.

W : Have you decided what kind of wine you' d like to have?
무슨 포도주를 드실 지 결정하셨어요?

G : Thank you. I don' t drink. 고맙습니다만, 전 술을 안마십니다.

스테이크를 주문할 때는 차림표를 참고하면 되고, "어떻게 익혀 드릴까요?"라는 질문은 종업원이 꼭 물어보는 질문이니 "well done 아주 바싹 익힌 것, medium 중간 정도 익힌 것, rare 설 익힌 것"을 참고하여 주문하면 된다. 드레싱의 종류로는 French, Italian, Thousand Island가 있는데 마요네즈에 파슬리, 피망, 삶은 달걀, 케첩을 다져 넣은 따우전 아일랜드가 비교적 한국인 입맛에 맞으니 선호하는 드레싱이 없을 때는 이것을 주문하면 된다.

Dialogue *C*

W : Waiter, G : Guest

W : How was your dinner?
식사는 어떠셨습니까?

G : **It was very good.**
아주 좋았습니다.

W : I'm glad. Would you like to have some coffee now?
다행이군요. 지금 커피를 드시겠어요?

G : **Yes, please.**
예, 주세요.

W : How about some dessert?
후식을 드시겠습니까?

G : **What would you suggest?**
뭐가 좋아요?

W : How about a piece of cheesecake? It's excellent.
치즈케이크가 어떻겠습니까? 아주 좋습니다.

G : **That sounds good.**
그거 좋을 것 같군요.

식사 후에 제공되는 후식으로는 한국과는 달리 케이크 등이 제공되니 선호하는 후식을 주문하면 되고, 어떤 종류의 후식이 있는지 알고 싶을 때는 "What kind of dessert do you have?"라고 질문하면 된다. 마땅히 선호하는 후식이 없을 때는 "What would you suggest?"라고 말하면 그 레스토랑에서 자신 있는 후식을 추천해 준다.

Dialogue *D*

W : Waiter, G : Guest

W : Good evening?
안녕하십니까?

G : Good evening. May I have the cocktail list?
안녕하십니까. 칵테일 리스트 좀 주세요.

W : Here it is. .... What would you like to drink?
여기 있습니다. 무엇을 드시겠습니까?

G : I want a glass of Whiskey on the rocks.
나는 얼음을 넣은 위스키를 마시겠습니다.

W : What brand do you want?
어떤 브랜드를 원하십니까?

G : Bourbon Whiskey.
버번 위스키요.

W : Would you like something to go with it?
안주도 드릴까요?

G : I' ll have Buffalo wings.
버팔로 닭 날개로 먹겠습니다.

W : OK. That will be $ 8:30.
좋습니다. 8달러 30센트입니다.

저녁 시간에 가볍게 한 잔 하기 위해서 칵테일 바를 이용하게 된다. 칵테일의 종류가 우리나라와 다르니 리스트를 참고하면 되고, 위스키나 코냑은 얼음이 필요하면 Whiskey(Cognac) on the rocks.라고 말하면 된다. 안주도 리스트를 참고해서 주문하는데, 닭고기의 경우 외국에선 날개가 다리보다 비싸니 참고해서 주문하면 된다.- Bourbon Whiskey : 미국 켄터키 주의 Bourbon 지방이 주산지인 옥수수 원료 위스키. Buffalo wings : 닭 날개를 튀겨 핫소스를 바른 양념 통닭.

Dialogue E

B : Bartender, G : Guest

B : Good evening?
안녕하십니까?

G : Good evening. May I have the cocktail list?
안녕하십니까. 칵테일 메뉴 좀 주세요.

B : Here it is. .... What will it be?
여기 있습니다. 무엇을 드시겠습니까?

G : A single shot of scotch, please.
스카치 한 잔 주세요.

B : On the rocks?
얼음을 넣어 드릴까요?

G : No, straight, please.
아니오, 그냥 주세요.

B : Coming right up.
손님, 즉시 갖다드리겠습니다.

저녁 시간에 술을 마시기 위해서 칵테일 바를 이용하게 된다. 위스키나 코냑을 주문하면 바텐더가 On the rocks, sir?(얼음을 넣어 드릴까요?)라고 물어보는데 필요하면 Yes, on the rocks, please.라고 대답하고, 그냥 마시고 싶으면 No, straight, please.(아니오, 그냥 주세요.)라고 말하면 된다. 스카치 같이 독한 술(hard liquor)의 작은 한잔은 a shot of scotch라고 말하며, 맥주 같이 약한 술의 한잔은 a glass of beer라고 말한다.

5 Role Play

Student A

A : 안녕하세요, 손님. 저는 피트라고 합니다. 저는 오늘 저녁에 손님들의 시중을 들 웨이터입니다. 포도주 목록이 여기 있습니다. 곧 돌아오겠습니다.
B : Thank you.

A : 주문하시겠습니까?
B : Yes.
A : 무얼 드시겠습니까?
B : I'll have a New York Steak.
A : 어떻게 해드릴까요?
B : Well done, please.
A : 구운 감자로 하시겠습니까, 밥으로 하시겠습니까?
B : Baked potato, please.
A : 수프입니까, 샐러드입니까?
B : Salad.
A : 드레싱은 뭐로 할까요?
B : Thousand Island.
A : 커피는 식사와 같이 드시겠습니까? 아니면 나중에 드시겠습니까?
B : Later.
A : 무슨 포도주를 하실 지 결정하셨어요?
B : Thank you. I don't drink.

A : 식사는 어떠셨습니까?
B : It was very good.
A : 다행이군요. 지금 커피를 드시겠어요?
B : Yes, please.
A : 후식을 드시겠습니까?
B : What would you suggest?
A : 치즈케이크가 어떻겠습니까? 아주 좋습니다.
B : That sounds good.

Student *B*

A : Good evening, sir. I' m Pete ; I' ll be your waiter this evening. Here is our wine list. I' ll be back shortly.

B : 감사합니다.

A : Are you ready to order?

B : 예.

A : What would you like to have?

B : 뉴욕 스테이크로 하겠습니다.

A : How would you like to have it?

B : 잘 익혀 주세요.

A : Baked potato or rice?

B : 구운 감자로 주세요.

A : Soup or salad?

B : 샐러드요.

A : What kind of dressing would you like?

B : 따우전 아일랜드로 주세요.

A : Would you like to have coffee with your meal or later?

B : 나중에요.

A : Have you decided what kind of wine you' d like to have?

B : 됐습니다. 전 술을 안마십니다.

A : How was your dinner?

B : 아주 좋았습니다.

A : I' m glad. Would you like to have some coffee now?

B : 예, 주세요.

A : How about some dessert?

B : 뭐가 좋아요?

A : How about a piece of cheesecake? It' s excellent.

B : 그거 좋을 것 같군요.

Unit 14 At the Fast Food Restaurant

1 Vocabulary and Patterns

* (french) fries 감자튀김
* coke coca cola 코카콜라

* Will that be all? 그게 전부인가요?

  That' s all(it). 그게 전부입니다.

* (For) here or to go? 여기서 드실 건가요? 가져가실 건가요?

EX

A : For here or to go?
B : To go.

* With everything on it? 다 얹어드릴까요?

EX

A : With everything on it?
B : Except onion. 양파는 빼고요.

* 핫도그를 주문할 때 점원이 전부 다 발라드릴까요? 라는 표현은 Would you like it with the works?이며 여기에서 the works는 속어로 전부, 모두라는 뜻이다.

EX

A : Would you like it with the works?
B : Yes, With everything on it.

2 Utterance-Response Drills

Would either of you care for a cocktail before dinner?

No, thank you. I think we're ready to order.

Are you ready to order?

Yes, what are your dinner specials tonight?

Are you going to have dessert?

I'll try the apple pie.

Did you order the sausage or ham?

I'm the ham.

May I warm up your coffee?

Please. That hits the spot this morning.

I'd like the tab, please.

You can pay at the counter.

Oh, okay. Thank you.

Would this be one check or separate?

One check, please.

Waitress, where do I pay the bill?

I can take care of it for you whenever you're ready.

3 Dialogue

Dialogue A

E : Employer, G : Guest

E : May I take your order? 주문하시겠습니까?

G : **Yes. I'd like three hamburgers.** 예, 햄버거 세 개 주세요.

E : With everything on it? 다 얹어드릴까요?

G : **Yes, except onion.** 예, 양파만 빼고 주세요.

E : Any (French) fries? 감자튀김은요?

G : **Yes, two orders.** 예, 2인분 주세요.

E : Anything to drink? 마실 것은요?

G : **Three large cokes, please.** 큰 사이즈로 콜라 세 잔이요.

E : Will that be all? 다 됐나요?

G : **That's all(it).** 다 됐습니다.

E : For here or to go? 여기서 드실 건가요? 가져가실 건가요?

G : **For here, please.** 여기서 먹을 겁니다.

E : OK. That will be $ 12. 30. 좋습니다. 12달러 30센트입니다.

햄버거를 구입할 때에 점원이 With everything on it?이라고 물어보는데 자신이 싫어하는 햄버거 재료가 있을 때는 Except ______ . 라고 대답하면 된다. 대부분의 패스트푸드점에서는 감자튀김도 판매하는데 1인분이면 one order. 2인분 이상이면 숫자 + orders. 라고 말하면 된다. (For) here or to go? 라는 질문에는 버스 여행 중 휴게실 등에서는 To go. 라고 이야기하면 차안에서 먹을 수 있도록 포장을 해준다.

Dialogue *B*

E : Employer, G : Guest

E : May I help you?
무엇을 도와드릴까요?

G : I'd like a hotdog and a medium coke with lots of ice.
핫도그 한 개와 얼음을 많이 넣은 중간 사이즈 콜라 한잔주세요.

E : OK. Would you like it with the works?
좋습니다. 전부 다 발라드릴까요?

G : Yes, with everything on it.
예, 다 발라주세요.

E : Will that be all?
이게 전부인가요?

G : That's all(it).
전부입니다.

E : For here or to go?
여기서 드실 건가요? 가져가실 건가요?

G : For here, please.
여기서 먹을 겁니다.

E : OK. That will be $ 9. 30.
좋습니다. 9달러 30센트입니다.

핫도그를 구입할 때에는 점원이 Would you like it with the works?이라고 물어보는데 다 발라주기를 원하면 Yes, with everything on it.(예, 다 발라주세요.)라고 대답하면 되고, 자신이 싫어하는 재료가 있을 때는 Except ____.라고 대답하면 된다. 콜라나 사이다를 주문할 때 얼음을 원하면 A coke(7-Up) with lots of ice.라고 이야기하고, 원하지 않으면 A coke with no ice.라고 말하면 된다.

Dialogue *C*

E : Employer, G : Guest

E : May I help you?
도와드릴까요?

G : Yes, give me two toasts and a large coke.
토스트 두 개와 큰 사이즈 콜라 한잔주세요.

E : Would you like butter on your toast?
토스트에 버터를 바르시겠어요?

G : Yes.
예, 발라주세요.

E : Will that be all?
이게 전부인가요?

G : That' s all(it).
전부입니다.

E : For here or to go?
여기서 드실 건가요? 가져가실 건가요?

G : For here, please.
여기서 먹을 겁니다.

later 잠시 후

G : I couldn' t finish this food. Can I have a doggie bag?
이것을 다 먹지 못했는데, 싸가지고 갈 봉지 하나 주시겠어요?

E : Here it is.
여기 있습니다.

패스트푸드점에서는 주로 햄버거, 핫도그, 토스트, 샌드위치와 콜라(coke) 등의 음료수를 판매한다. 식당 안에서 먹고 남은 음식을 싸가지고 가고 싶을 때는 Would you wrap this for me?(이것 좀 싸주시겠어요?)라고 말하던지, Can I have a doggie bag? (싸가지고 갈 봉지 하나 주시겠어요?)라고 말하면 된다. doggie bag은 먹다 남은 음식을 봉지에 싸가지고 가서 개에게 준다는 의미에서 유래되었다.

4 Role Play

Student 𝔄

A : 차림표 좀 주세요.

B : We don't have menus. Everything's on that sign behind the counter.

A : 아, 미안해요. 그걸 못 봤군. 음... 큰 치즈버거하나하고 양파 튀김 하고요.

B : Anything to drink?

A : 커피만 줘요. 설탕은 타고, 크림은 넣지 말아요.

B : Sure. Just a minute.

A : 어서 오세요. 웬디스입니다. 오늘은 무엇으로 드시겠어요?

B : I will have a cheeseburger and a small coke.

A : 여기서 드실 건가요, 가지고 가실 건가요?

B : Here.

A : 어서 오세요. 하디스입니다. 오늘은 뭐로 드시겠습니까?

B : I'll have a double bacon cheeseburger with extra pickles and ketchup on the side.

A : 5분만 기다리세요. 기다리실 수 있죠?

B : No, not at all. Please bring it out to me.

Student *B*

A : Could I get a menu, please?

B : 차림표는 없습니다. 계산대 뒤의 차림표에 다 적혀 있습니다.

A : Oh, sorry, I didn't see it. Uh... Can I have a large cheeseburger, please, and an order of onion rings?

B : 마실 것은요?

A : Just coffee – with sugar. No cream.

B : 알겠습니다. 잠깐만 기다리십시오.

A : Welcome to Wendy's. What can I get you today?

B : 치즈버거 한 개와 콜라 작은 것 하나 주세요.

A : Here or to go?

B : 여기서 먹을 겁니다.

A : Hi. Welcome to Hardee's. What can I get you today?

B : 더블 베이컨 치즈버거를 주시는데 피클을 좀 더 넣어 주시고요, 케첩을 따로 담아 주세요.

A : That will be about five minutes. Do you mind waiting?

B : 그럼요. 나오면 저한테 갖다 주세요.

Unit

15 At a Barber's Shop

1 Vocabulary and Patterns

* crewcut 스포츠 머리 / bangs (단발머리의) 앞머리 wear one's hair banged 앞머리를 가지런히 깍다.

EX

Please don't cut my bangs too short.
앞머리는 너무 짧게 자르지 마세요

* get a perm = have one's hair permed 파마를 하다.
* hair coloring = dyeing one's hair 염색을 하다.

* trim 다듬다 / shortcut = get a short hair cut 짧게 자르다.(TEPS Voca Part I)

EX

A : How would you like your hair cut? 어떻게 깎아드릴까요?
B : I just want a ________ . 조금만 다듬어 주세요

(a) shortcut (b) shortwave (c) tidy up (d) trim

★d

* part (머리를) 가르마 타다. – He has his hair parted in the middle.(한가운데서) / at the side.(옆에서)

EX

A : Where do you want your hair parted? 가리마를 어떻게 타드릴까요?
B : On the left. 왼쪽으로요.

1. 기본 동사 Get의 주요 패턴 하나

일차적으로 get은 구체적인 사물뿐만 아니라 추상적인 것이나 어떤 동작을 얻거나 받을 때 사용되는 데 주로 「get + a + 명사」의 패턴으로 쓰인다.

get a letter 편지를 받다.
get a present 선물을 받다.
get a haircut 이발하다.
get a shave 이발사가 자기에게 면도를 해주다.
get a shoeshine 타인이 자기의 구두를 닦아주다.
get a divorce 이혼을 얻다 → 이혼하다.
get a raise 봉급을 인상되다.
get a refund 돈을 되돌려 받다.
get a promotion 승진 또는 진급하다.
get a discount 할인을 하다.
get a cold 감기를 얻다 → 감기에 걸리다.
get a headache 두통을 얻다 → 두통이 있다.
get the flu 유행성 독감에 걸리다.
get the hiccups 딸꾹질이 나다.

2 Utterance-Response Drills

How would you like your hair cut?

I want to cut it short.

How short?

To about mid ear.

How would you like your hair cut?

Just trim and taper, please.

Okay. No problem.

Don't cut it too short.

What kind of style would you like?

I brought a picture. Can you cut it like this?

What kind of style would you like?

Please set my hair in the same style.

What style do you think is the best for me?

How about getting a perm?

I want to get a shampoo.

Okay. Please have a seat.

Well, I was thinking of getting a perm as well.

Okay. Let's give you a shampoo first.

I'd like a manicure.

Sure. Let's remove the old polish first.

What colors do you have?

All of these here. Take your pick.

3 Role Play

Student A

A : 다음이 제 차례인가요?

B : Yes, it'll just be a few minutes.

〈After a while〉

B : Right this way. Please sit here.

A : 감사합니다. 머리를 깎고 샴푸해 주세요.

B : How would you like it cut?

A : 위를 고르고 옆을 다듬어 주세요.

B : Please step this way for your shampoo.

A : 저는 비듬이 많으니 잘 문질러 주세요.

B : May I put some pomade on?

A : 예, 약간만.

B : Where do you want your hair parted?

A : 왼쪽으로 해주세요.

A : 머리 결이 숱이 많고 푸석푸석하군요. 손질을 해야겠는데요.

B : How much is it for hair treatment and a cut?

A : 30달러입니다.

B : How about a perm?

A : 모두 합쳐서요? 그러면 약 100달러쯤 됩니다.

B : Not bad. Let's do it all.

Student *B*

A : Am I next?

B : 몇 분만 있으면 되겠습니다.

〈잠시 후〉

B : 이쪽으로 오시죠. 앉으세요.

A : Thank you. A haircut and a shampoo, please.

B : 어떤 형으로 깎아 드릴까요?

A : Even out the top and trim the sides, please.

B : 이쪽으로 오셔서 머리를 감으시죠.

A : I have a lot of dandruff. Please give my hair a good scrub.

B : 포마드를 발라드릴까요?

A : Yes, but not too much.

B : 가르마를 어떻게 해드릴까요?

A : On the left.

A : Your hair is very thick and dry. You need a hair treatment.

B : 머리를 손질하고 자르는데 얼마입니까?

A : Thirty dollars.

B : 파마하는데는 얼마입니까?

A : For everything? That would be about $100.

Unit 16 At the Post Office and Bank

1 Vocabulary and Patterns

* roll 100장 단위의 우표

EX

A : May I have a roll of 32-cent stamps?
B : Sure.

* airmail 항공우편 / surface mail 선박우편

* regular mail 보통우편 / special delivery, express delivery(영국) 속달우편 / registered mail 등기우편

EX

A : I'd like to send this by special delivery.
registered mail
airmail
surface mail
B : Where to?
A : To Seoul, Korea. How long will it take?
B : It will take about five days.

* bank teller 은행직원

  personal teller 개인계좌 담당 직원

  merchant teller 상업계좌 담당 직원

* ATM(Automatic Teller Machine) 현금 자동인출기

* in singles 1달러짜리로

EX

A : How would you like that? 어떻게 드릴까요?
B : I want it all in singles. 모두 1달러짜리로 주셨으면 좋겠습니다.

* account 예금계좌

  I'd like to open a savings account, please.

* deposit 예금하다, 예치하다

  I want to deposit 500 dollars. = I'd like to make a deposit of 500 dollars.

* withdraw (돈을)인출하다

  I want to withdraw 100 dollars, please.

* exchange rate 환율

EX

A : What's the current exchange rate?
What's today's exchange rate?
B : It's 1,200 won to a dollar.

* I'd like to cash some travelers checks, please.

* break [change] 바꾸다.

Can you break [change] a twenty dollar bill?

= Do you have change for a twenty?

= Could I have change for a twenty?

* I'd like to change these dollars.

유용한 표현들

우체국 · 은행에서 ...

① Excuse me. Where can I buy stamps?
실례합니다만 우표를 어디서 사는 거죠?

② I'd like to send a letter to Korea.
편지 한 통을 한국으로 부치고 싶습니다.

③ What's the airmail postage to Korea?
한국까지 항공우편 요금은 얼마입니까?

④ Please give me ten twenty cent stamps.
20센트짜리 우표 10장 주세요.

⑤ I want to send this letter by special delivery.
이 편지를 속달로 부치고 싶은데요.

⑥ Do you handle parcel post?
소포우편물을 여기서 취급합니까?

⑦ I'd like to cash this check.
이 수표를 현금으로 바꾸고 싶습니다.

⑧ Give me the whole amount in ten-dollar bills.
전액을 10달러짜리로 주세요.

⑨ Where can I exchange American dollars for won?
어디서 달러를 원화로 바꿀 수 있을까요?

⑩ What's today's exchange rate?
오늘의 환율은 어떻습니까?

2 Patterns Drill

(1) I'd like to change a hundred dollar bill.

Can you change ?

break

Do you have change for a hundred

Could I

(2) How much is airmail to Korea?

L.A

Toronto

Manila

(3) I'd like to send this by special delivery.

registered mail

airmail

surface mail

3 Utterance-Response Drills

How much is airmail to Korea?

For a regular size letter?

Yes. It's very light.

That will be fifty cents for airmail.

I'd like to send this letter by registered mail.

Where to?

To New York. How long will it take?

It will take one or two days.

How much is the postage on this?

It will be $2.25.

What if I send it by express mail?

Then it would cost you $20.00.

I'd like to cash this check, please.

Okay. Please endorse it on the back. How would you like it?

Give it to me in large bills.

Where can I exchange American dollars to won?

Over at the next counter.

Thank you. Over there?

Yes. She will help you.

What's the exchange rate?

As of today it's 900won to the dollar.

Okay. Then I would like to change $500.

First, may I see your passport?

4 Role Play

Student A

A : 이 소포를 한국에 보내려고 합니다.

B : All right. Let me weigh it. Is it by ship?

A : 아뇨. 항공편입니다. 항공편으로는 한국에 며칠 만에 도착합니까?

B : It takes about 5 days, I think. What are the contents?

A : 기념품들인데요, 넥타이, 인형, 만년필 같은 것들입니다.

B : Will you fill out this customs declaration form? Your name and address, the contents, the receiver's name and address, and prices.

A : 예. 봉함엽서 있습니까?

B : Yes, we do. How many do you want?

A : 2장만 주세요.

B : You can't enclose anything in it.

A : 한국의 부산에 전보를 보내고 싶습니다.

B : Yes. Please write down the message here.

A : 전보요금은 어떻게 합니까?

B : 50 cents per word to Korea.

A : 한 단어 당 50센트라고요? 내가 생각한 것보다 훨씬 비싸군요.

B : But as you know, "LT" will make it cheaper.

A : 가만있자... 그러면 "서신전보"로 하겠습니다.

Student B

A : I would like to send this parcel to Korea.

B : 알겠습니다. 무게를 달아봅시다. 배편으로 보내실 겁니까?

A : No, by airmail. How long does it take to reach Korea by airmail?

B : 약 5일 정도 걸릴 겁니다. 내용물은 무엇입니까?

A : Souvenirs such as ties, dolls, and fountain pens.

B : 이 세관 신고서에 기입하여 주시겠습니까? 성함과 주소, 내용물, 수취인 성함과 주소, 그리고 가격을 기입하시면 됩니다.

A : Yes. Do you have any aerograms?

B : 예, 있습니다. 몇 장이 필요하십니까?

A : Just two, please.

B : 안에는 어떤 것도 동봉할 수 없습니다.

A : I want to send a telegram to Busan, Korea.

B : 알겠습니다. 전하실 말을 여기다 써주세요.

A : What is the telegram charge?

B : 한국까지는 한 단어 당 50센트입니다.

A : 50 cents per word? It's more expensive than I expected.

B : 아시겠지만, "서신정보"는 값이 더 쌀 겁니다.

A : Let me see... I'll make it "LT", then.

Unit 17

Health

1 Vocabulary and Patterns

1. 신체의 아픔을 표현하기

① -ache를 쓰는 경우

I have a headache.(두통) / a migraine (headache).(편두통)

a toothache.(치통) / a stomachache.(위통)

a backache.(요통)

EX

A : I have a serious migraine _______ today. 나는 오늘 편두통이 심해요.

B : Whenever I have pain throbbing inside my skull, I can't concentrate on anything at all.(TEPS Vocab. Part I)

머리 안에서 두드리는 것 같은 고통이 있을 때마다 저는 전혀 일에 집중할 수가 없어요.

(a) pain (b) stomachache

(c) headache (d) toothache

② sore를 쓰는 경우

I have a sore eye.(눈이 아픈)

a sore throat.(목이 따끔거리는)

a sore arm.(팔이 쑤시는)

③ pain을 쓰는 경우

I have a pain in my side.(옆구리의 통증)

in my shoulder.(어깨의 저림)

in my knee.(무릎이 쑤심)

④ 기타

I have a stiff neck.(목이 뻣뻣해요.)

I have stiff shoulders.(어깨가 뻐근해요.)

I have a runny nose.(콧물이 나요.)

I have diarrhea.(설사해요.)

EX

Q : You look pale [tired]. What's the matter?
You don't look very well. What's wrong with you?
How are you feeling today?
How do you feel today?
What seems to be the problem [trouble]?
How did you break your arm?

A : I have a cold [headache, cough, sore throat].
I have a high temperature.
I have a fever and runny nose.
I have high blood pressure.
I've got a terrible pain in my neck [back, knee, stomach].
I've got a heart problem [a bad case of athlete's foot].
I ache all over.

2 Patterns Drill

(1) You look happy.
tired
healthy
sleepy

(2) What's wrong?
the matter
up
happening

(3) How are you feeling today?
they
is he
she

(4) I have a cold.
a bad cough
a headache
a stomachache
a sore throat

(5) I've broken my arm.
scratched my finger
injured my knee
hurt my shoulder

3 Utterance-Response Drills

You've got a funny look on your face.

Yeah, my stomach is upset.

How was Taekwondo practice?

Awful. I have aches and pains all over.

I can't go another step.

Come on. We've got to reach safety.

No, my feet are killing me.

Where's the pain?

Right in the back of my head.

You should lie down for a while.

You should like you have a cold.

Yes. I have a terrible headache.

Do you have any allergies?

Not that I know of.

How do you feel today?

I feel much better than yesterday.

I've got something in my eyes.

Let me see.

I've got the runs.

What did you eat yesterday.

4 Role Play

Student A

A : 몸이 불편해 보이는데.

B : I am. I feel simply awful.

A : 그래, 어디가 아픈 거야?

B : Well, my stomach is upset, and I have aches and pains all over.

A : 그럼 집에 가보는 게 좋겠군.

B : Yeah, I'm taking the day off.

A : 그래, 오늘은 좀 어때?

B : Great! Last night I slept like a baby.

A : 보기에도 더 좋아 보이는군.

B : Thank you.

A : 종합병원입니다. 뭘 도와드릴까요?

B : Yes. This is an emergency.

A : 잘 알겠습니다. 저에게 상황을 설명해주시고, 당신이 있는 위치, 성함 그리고 전화번호를 알려주세요.

B : I'm sorry. I didn't understand that. Could you repeat that, please?

A : 예. 무슨 일이 일어났는지 저에게 말씀해 주세요.

B : My roommate is very sick. He is vomiting, has a fever, and aches all over.

A : 알았습니다. 살모넬라인 것 같습니다.

B : Pardon? I didn't catch that last part.

A : 살모넬라라고 했습니다. 식중독 말이지요. 자, 이제 당신의 주소를 말씀해 주세요.

B : We're in Room 508 of the Essex Hotel at 2532 Simpson Avenue.

A : 알겠습니다. 당신의 친구를 눕혀 놓으시면 앰뷸런스가 곧 갈 것입니다.

Student *B*

A : You look like you're feeling under the weather.

B : 그래. 굉장히 안 좋아.

A : So, where's the pain?

B : 그저, 배가 아프고, 온몸이 쑤셔.

A : You should go home then.

B : 그래, 오늘 하루 쉬려고 해.

A : So, how do you feel today?

B : 아주 좋아! 어젯밤엔 잠도 푹 잘 잤어.

A : You look better, too.

B : 고마워.

A : General Hospital. May I help you?

B : 예. 긴급한 일입니다.

A : All right, sir. Please tell me the nature of the emergency, where you are, your name and telephone number.

B : 미안합니다. 무슨 말인지 잘 모르겠습니다. 다시 한 번 말씀해주시겠습니까?

A : Yes, sir. Tell me what happened.

B : 제 룸메이트가 굉장히 아픕니다. 토하고, 열도 나고, 그리고 안 쑤시는 데가 없답니다.

A : I see. That could be salmonella.

B : 뭐라고요? 마지막 부분이 무슨 말인지 모르겠습니다.

A : "Salmonella." That's food poisoning. Now please give me your address.

B : 심슨街 2532번지에 있는 에섹스 호텔 508호에 있습니다.

A : All right. Have your friend lie down and an ambulance will be on the way immediately.

Unit 18 Sightseeing

1 Vocabulary and Patterns

관광통역가이드 기출문제

* In bound 외국인에 의한 국내여행
  Out bound 내국인에 의한 해외여행
* Package Tour 교통, 숙박, 관광 등 모든 것이 포함된 전 일정 여행
* Chart Tour 전세여행 / Incentive Tour 포상여행
* Over Land Tour 통과상륙여행 - 동일 국가 내에서 A기항지에서 B기항지로 이동하면서 통과상륙의 허가를 얻어 3~7일 정도의 여행을 하고 그 선박에 다시 승선하는 여행을 말한다.
* Shore Excursion 기항지 상륙여행
* SIT(Special Interest Tour) 고객의 관심을 유도하기 위하여 특별한 테마를 가지고 기획, 운영하는 여행
* Technical Visit 산업시찰여행
* PVS(Passport. Visa. Shot-예방접종)
* ASTA(American Society of Travel Agents) 1931년에 창립되어 미주에 본부를 두고 있는 미주 여행자협회
* WTO(World Tourism Organization) 스페인 마드리드에 본부가 있고 정부 관광기관(우리나라는 문화관광부)이 회원으로 되어있는 세계관광기구

* PATA(Pacific Asia Travel Association) 1951년에 하와이 관광국의 제창으로 창립되고 샌프란시스코에 본부가 있는 태평양 아시아 관광협회

유용한 표현들

* Where would you suggest I go for interesting places?
* We' d like to see Mt. Jirisan National Park.
* What will we see next?
* The bus will be here at 9 and we' ll leave at 9:30.
* Have you ever been here before?
* First we go Kyungkijon(Shrine), then Pungnammun(Gate).
* Would you give us some information about that building?
  It' s Jeonju Gaeksa, guest house. This was built in early years of Josen dynasty.
* Let' s take a picture with the view of that building.
* How was your trip to Korea?

2 Patterns Drill

(1) We'd like to see Mt. Dobongsan.
the interesting places
Mt. Maisan and Tapsa
the World Cup Stadium

(2) Do you know what that building is?
house
school
shop

(3) Will you take my picture with a view of that building?
river
mountain
house
lake

(4) I had a wonderful time there.
good
great
lot of fun

3 Utterance-Response Drills

A. General Sightseeing(일반관광)

Dialogue A

A : Excuse me, officer. I'm looking for the Tourist Information Center. Would you help me?

B : Yes. The Tourist Information Center of Jeolla Province is located at Gosa-dong.

A : Do you happen to know the telephone number?

B : Yes, I do. It's 288-0105.

Dialogue B

A : We'd like to see World Cup Stadium.

B : We run three motor coach tours daily.

A : Do you think we have to reserve seats in advance?

B : No. First come, first served.

Dialogue C

A : May I help you?

B : Yes, I'd like to rent a car.

A : May I see your International Drivers License and passport?

B : Here they are. Can you tell me the rental charge?

Dialogue D

A : Do you know what that building is?

B : That' s City-Hall.

A : Will you take my picture with the view of that building?

B : I' d be glad to.

Dialogue E

A : How was your trip to Jeolla Province?

B : I had a wonderful time there.

A : What impressed you the most?

B : The kindness and beautiful scenery. Especially, citizens in North Jeolla Province are very kind.

B. Jeonju Vicinity

Dialogue A

A : Where would you suggest I go for interesting places near Jeonju?

B : What are you interested in?

A : I think it' s a Buddhist temple.

B : How about Gumsansa Temple? It' s famous for Mirukjeon Hall. It is the uniquely designed three-story main hall within the precincts of Gumsansa Temple.

Dialogue *B*

A : I wish to go to the Jeonju museum. Would you please tell me how I can get there?

B : There is the sightseeing bus for the museum. It is very convenient for tourists.

A : Where can I get on the bus?

B : In front of Jeonju City-Hall.

Dialogue *C*

A : We are now passing by Pungnammun Gate, the south gate of the four gates of Jeonju.

B : It looks very old. When was it constructed?

A : It was built in 1389, the first year of King Gongyang of Goryeo dynasty. But this present one was built in 1767. The style of the gate is unique in that the pillars extend up through the second story to the supports of the roof.

Dialogue *D*

A : I'd like to have sea food. Could you recommend a good restaurant?

B : There's a good restaurant in Gunsan.

A : How long does it take from here?

B : About one hour by car.

Dialogue *E*

A : I'm interested in calligraphy.

B : Why don't you visit Gangam Calligraphy Institute? This is the only calligraphy museum in Korea.

A : How many works are there in the institute?

B : It displays 1,162 works, including the masterpieces of outstanding calligraphers, painters, and scholars.

C. The Jirisan-Deokyusan Vicinity

Dialogue *A*

A : I want to climb the mountain. Is there any good mountain in Jeolla Province?

B : I think it's Mt. Jirisan. Mt. Jirisan, which stretches into three provinces, was the first area in Korea to be designated a national park.

A : How can I get there?

B : You can take the bus and it'll take 2 hours.

Dialogue *B*

A : Would you tell me how I can get to Muju Resort?

B : There is the sightseeing bus leaving for Muju at city-Hall every 30 minutes.

A : Is there any good hotel?

B : Yes, there is. Muju Resort is Asia's largest recreation and sport resort with a super deluxe hotel. The name is the Hotel Tirol.

Dialogue C

A : That is Mt. Maisan. "Maisan" means the horse-ear mountain.

B : Yes. You mean the name of the mountain is derived from the appearance of its twin peaks, right?

A : Yes, it is. And within the park there is Tapsa Temple, which contains 80 unique conical pagodas of piled-up stones at the foot of Mt. Maisan.

B : They are very marvelous.

Dialogue D

A : What's that building?

B : It's Gwanghallu Pavilion. Here Chunhyang and Lee Doryung were smitten with love for each other. Chunhyang Festival is held every year.

A : Who are Chunhyang and Lee Doryung?

B : This site is famous for the story of Chunhyang, a chaste and faithful woman of the Joseon Dynasty, and her lover Lee Doryung. Their story is sometimes called "the Korean Romeo and Juliet."

Dialogue E

A : What is that root resembling a human body?

B : It is Ginseng, a medical herb. Recently, clinical studies of Ginseng have indicated it has many beneficial effects.

A : Come to think of it, I remember it has anti-cancer properties.

B : Yes, you're right. In addition, it helps protect and heal the liver, and improve the function of stomach and brain.

D. Naejangsan–Byonsan Course

Dialogue A

A : What is Mt. Naejang famous for?

B : It is well-known for maple leaves. At Mt. Naejang, more than 30 kinds of maple trees stand on both sides of the road. Mt. Naejang is especially scenic during late October and early November when the fall foliage is at its peak.

A : Where is it?

B : It is located near Jeongup city in Jeollabuk-do. It will take about one hour from Jeonju.

Dialogue B

A : I'd like to go to the beach.

B : Why don't you go to Byunsan Beach Resort. Beside the beach, there are so many interesting places ; Naeso Temple, Jikso Waterfall, Chaeseokgang Beach and so on.

A : How long will it take to go there?

B : It'll take about one and half hours by car.

Dialogue C

A : Mr. Brown, on your left you can see Gochangupseong.

B : It's very old. When was it constructed?

A : This fortress was constructed in 1453, the first year of reign of King Danjong of the Joseon Dynasty.

B : It's very interesting that they used all untrimmed rocks to build this fortress.

Dialogue *D*

A : What will we see next?

B : We're on our way to Mt. Seonun.

A : Can you tell me in advance what we'll see?

B : Of course. It is famous for a spectacular view, 500-year old camellia trees and the grilled eel dish.

Dialogue *E*

A : What is that statue?

B : It's a bronze statue of General Jeon Bong-jun.

A : What are his contributions?

B : He started a revolution in order to protect people groaned under misgovernment of the late Joseon dynasty.

4 Dialogue

Dialogue A

G : Guide, T : Tourist

G : Good morning. May I help you?
안녕하세요. 무엇을 도와드릴까요?

T : Yes, I'd like to see some city sights. Would you suggest some interesting places to visit in this city?
예, 시내 관광을 하고 싶습니다. 이 도시에서 구경할 만한 곳을 추천해주시겠습니까?)

G : Sure. It's a sightseeing bus of the city. It'll take you by all the major points of interest.
물론이지요. 시내 관광버스가 있습니다. 여행사에서 흥미 있는 모든 주요장소로 태워다 줄 것입니다.

T : How much is it?
요금이 얼마입니까?

G : It's $15 per person for a two-hour tour.
2시간 관광에 1인당 15달러입니다.

T : What time does the next tour leave?
다음 관광은 몇 시에 출발합니까?

G : It leaves at 10 a.m..
10시에 출발합니다.

개인적으로 여행하는 지역의 도시를 관광할 때는 현지 여행사의 관광 프로그램에 참여하는 것이 좋다. 이럴 경우에는 가까운 관광 안내소에 가서 안내를 받으면 되고, 관광 안내소의 위치를 알고 싶을 때는 "Where is the tourist information?(관광 안내소가 어디에 있습니까?)"라고 말하고, 안내소에서 그 도시의 안내 팸플릿을 달라고 할 때에는 "Can I have a sightseer's pamphlet?(관광안내 팸플릿 하나 주시겠어요?)"라고 말한다.

Dialogue *B*

T : Tourist, P : Passerby

T : Excuse me.
실례합니다.

P : Yes.
네

T : Would you mind taking a picture of us?
사진 한 장 찍어 주시겠습니까?

P : What am I supposed to do?
어떻게 찍으면 됩니까?

T : Well, it's a simple automatic camera. All you have to do is aim and shoot.
아, 그것은 간단한 자동카메라예요. 그냥 초점을 잘 맞춰서 누르시기만 하면 됩니다.

P : Is that all?
그렇게만 하면 됩니까?

T : Yes, it's very simple.
네, 매우 간단합니다.

P : Say cheese.
치즈 해보세요.

T : Thank you very much.
대단히 감사합니다.

P : You are welcome.
천만예요.

사진을 찍어 달라고 부탁할 때 혼자일 때에는 Would you mind taking a picture of me?라고 말하며, 자동카메라 일 경우에는 It's a simple automatic camera. All you have to do is aim and shoot. (그것은 간단한 자동카메라예요. 그냥 초점을 잘 맞춰서 누르시기만 하면 됩니다.)라고 말하면 된다. 우리나라에서는 사진을 찍을 때 김치라고 말하지만, 영어권 사람들은 Say cheese.라고 말한다.

Dialogue *C*

T : Tourist, P : Passerby

T : Excuse me, Would you please take a picture for us?
실례합니다. 저희들 사진 좀 찍어 주시겠습니까?

P : **Sure, Where would you like to stand?**
물론이지요. 어디에 서시겠습니까?

T : We'll stand in front of the statue over there.
우리는 저기 동상 앞에 서 있겠습니다.

P : **What am I supposed to do?**
어떻게 찍으면 됩니까?

T : You can just push this button.
이 셔터를 누르시기만 하면 됩니다.

P : **All right. Say cheese.**
알겠습니다. 치즈 해보세요.

T : Thank you very much.
대단히 감사합니다.

P : **You are welcome.**
천만예요.

외국인에게 사진을 찍어 달라고 부탁할 때는 "Excuse me. Would you Would you please take a picture for us(me)? (실례합니다. 저희들 사진 좀 찍어 주시겠습니까?)라고 말하며, 자동카메라 일 경우에는 It's a simple automatic camera. You can just push this button.(그것은 간단한 자동카메라예요. 이 셔터를 누르시기만 하면 됩니다.)라고 말하면 된다. 외국인과 사진을 같이 찍고 싶을 때는 "Would you pose with me?"(저와 함께 사진을 찍으시겠습니까?)라고 말한다.

Dialogue D

T : Tourist, G : Guide

G : What do you want to see here in Los Angeles?
로스앤젤레스에서 무엇을 구경하고 싶으십니까?

T : I don't know. I need some information. Would you please recommend some interesting places to visit?
잘 모르겠습니다. 정보가 필요합니다. 구경할 만한 곳을 추천해 주시겠습니까?

G : Sure. You should go to the Getty Museum. You can see a collection of L.A's finest art.
물론이지요. 게티 박물관을 가보십시오. L.A의 가장 멋진 미술작품들을 구경할 수 있습니다.

T : I can hardly wait to see it?
그곳을 빨리 구경하고 싶군요.

G : The place is worth a visit.
그곳은 한번쯤 가볼만한 곳입니다.

T : What time does the Getty Museum close?
게티 박물관은 몇 시에 문을 닫습니까?

G : I think it's closes at 6 o'clock.
6시에 닫을 겁니다.

T : Thank you for your information.
정보를 주셔서 감사합니다.

G : You're welcome.
천만에요.

방문한 도시의 관광정보를 알고 싶을 때는 가까운 관광 안내소에 가서 안내를 받으면 된다. 유명한 건물이나 공원 등이 관광코스에 많이 포함되어 있지만 박물관이나 극장, 프로야구장도 관광객들이 선호하는 장소이다. 시간을 내어 미술작품이나 뮤지컬 한 편을 감상하는 것도 오래 기억에 남는 여행이 될 수 있을 것 같다.

Dialogue *E*

T : Tourist, C : Clerk

C : May I help you?
도와드릴까요?

T : Two adults for "Titanic" for the two-thirty showing, please?
2시 30분에 상영하는 "타이타닉"표 어른 2장 주세요.

C : Sorry, the two-thirty show is sold out.
죄송합니다만 2시30분표는 매진되었습니다.

T : Well. What about the next show?
그러면 다음에 상영하는 것은 어떻습니까?

C : Yes, I do have tickets for the six o'clock show.
네, 6시에 상영하는 표는 있습니다.

T : OK. Two adults, please. How much is it?
좋습니다. 어른 2장 주세요. 얼마입니까?

C : Fifteen dollars. Seven-fifty each.
1인당 7달러 50센트씩, 15달러입니다.

T : Here it is.
여기 있습니다.

Dialogue F

R : Rental, C : Clerk

R : May I help you?
무엇을 도와드릴까요?

T : Yes, I 'd like to rent a mid-sized car.
네, 중형차를 한 대 빌리고 싶습니다.

R : When do you need it?
차는 언제 필요하십니까?

T : I' d like to pick it up right now if possible.
가능하면 지금 바로 렌트하고 싶습니다.

R : All right. We have a Ford Taurus and a Mercury Sable available. Which one would you like?
좋습니다. 지금 "포드 토러스"와 "머큐리 세이블"이 있는데 어느 차로 하시겠습니까?

T : I' ll take a Mercury Sable. What' s your rate?
"머큐리 세이블"로 하겠습니다. 요금은 얼마입니까?

R : $ 40 plus a CDLW of $11 a day.
하루에 40달러이고 선택사항인 CDLW는 11달러입니다.

T : What' s CDLW?
CDLW가 무엇입니까?

R : It stands for Collision Damage and Loss Waiver. In the event of a Collision or theft, the insurance will cover the damage or loss of the vehicle.
그것은 충돌피해 및 손실보상면제의 약자입니다. 차가 도난당하거나 접촉사고가 날 경우, 보험회사가 자동차의 피해 보상을 하는 것입니다.

단체여행 중 하루정도 자유시간이 주어졌을 때 렌터카(rent-a-car)를 빌려서 주변지역을 돌아보면 현지인들의 생활 모습과 풍물을 몸소 체험해 볼 수 있다. 만약의 사고에 대비하여 Collision Damage and Loss Waiver(충돌피해 및 손실보상면제 : 렌터 기간 동안 한시적으로 가입하는 자동차 보험) 보험에 꼭 가입하는 게 좋다.

Dialogue G

R : Rental, C : Clerk

R : Hi. May I help you?
안녕하세요. 무엇을 도와드릴까요?

T : Yes, I 'd like to rent a car.
네, 차를 한 대 빌리고 싶습니다.

R : What kind of car do you want?
어떤 차종을 원하십니까?

T : May I have your brochure?
팸플릿 좀 보여주시겠습니까?

R : Here you are.
여기 있습니다.

T : (Pause) I' ll take this one.
이걸로 하겠습니다.

R : OK. May I see your driver' s license?
좋습니다. 면허증을 보여주시겠습니까?

T : Here is my international driver' s license.
여기 국제운전면허증이 있습니다.

R : OK. Do you have a credit card?
좋습니다. 신용카드를 가지고 있습니까?

T : Yes, here it is.
네, 여기 있습니다.

렌터카(rent-a-car)를 빌릴 때는 국제운전면허증과 신용카드는 꼭 소지해야 한다. 일부 지역에서는 국제운전면허증뿐만 아니라 국내 면허증도 보여 줄 것을 요구하니 두개를 소지하는 것이 좋고, 요금지불은 꼭 신용카드를 요구하니 외국에서 사용할 수 있는 VISA나 MASTER 카드를 소지해야 한다. 연료는 가득 채워서 빌려주고, 연료가 남으면 사용한 연료비만 내면 된다. 차량의 반납은 렌터카 사무소가 있는 곳이면 어디에서나 반납이 가능하다.

Dialogue *H*

T : Tourist, G : Guide

T : I want to see a Major League baseball game.
메이저리그 야구경기를 보고 싶습니다.

G : There is a game this Sunday.
이번 주 일요일에 경기가 있어요.

T : Which teams are playing?
어느 팀이 경기를 합니까?

G : Los Angeles Dodgers and San Francisco Giants.
LA 다저스와 샌프란시스코 자이언츠입니다.

T : Can I buy tickets now?
지금 입장권을 살 수 있습니까?

G : No. I think they are sold out. But don't worry. I've got two tickets.
안될 거예요. 매진됐을 겁니다. 하지만 걱정 마세요. 제가 입장권을 두 장 가지고 있으니까요.

T : Really? Thank you very much.
정말이에요? 대단히 감사합니다.

Dialogue 1

T : Tourist, C : Clerk

C : Do you know how to ride a jet ski?
제트 스키를 타실 줄 아십니까?

T : Of course, it's my favorite sport.
물론이지요, 제가 좋아하는 운동입니다.

C : Would you give me some tips on how to ride a jet ski?
제트 스키를 탈 때 필요한 규칙을 좀 알려주시겠습니까?

C : Sure. First you always wear a U.S coast Guard Approved personal flotation device when you ride a jet ski. Second ride only in daytime hours. Third know the rules of the road and never drink and ride.
물론이지요. 첫 번째 제트 스키를 탈 때는 항상 미국해안경비대가 승인한 개인구명조끼를 입어야 합니다. 두 번째 낮 시간에만 제트스키를 탈것. 세 번째 운전 법규를 준수하고 음주 운전을 하지 말 것입니다.

T : Sounds like the rules for driving a car.
자동차의 운전법규와 비슷한 것 같군요.

C : Yes, it's pretty much like that, except you ride it on the water.
네, 물위에서 탄다는 것만 제외하고는 거의 같습니다.

괌, 사이판, 하와이 등 해변이 많은 지역을 여행할 때에는 제트스키 등 수상 스포츠를 즐길 수 있는 기회가 많다. 수상 스포츠를 이용할 때는 될 수 있으면 호텔이나 현지 외국인들이 운영하는 시설을 이용하면 저렴하게 이용할 수 있으며, 일부 호텔에서는 자유이용권을 구입하면 투숙하는 기간 동안 무제한으로 여러 장비를 이용할 수 있다. 제트스키 등 조금은 위험한 장비를 이용할 때는 사전에 규칙 및 주의사항을 숙지하고 이용해야 한다.

Dialogue J

T : Tourist, O : Officer

O : Do you have a fishing license?
낚시 허가증을 소지하고 있습니까?

T : No, do I need one to fish?
아니오. 허가증이 필요합니까?

O : Yes, it's against the law to fish here without a license.
네, 이곳에서 허가증 없이 낚시하는 것은 위법입니다.

T : I'm sorry, I didn't know that.
죄송합니다, 몰랐습니다.

O : I'm sorry, too, but I have to give you a ticket for the violation.
저도 유감입니다만, 법규위반으로 티켓을 끊어야겠습니다.

T : How much is the fine?
벌금이 얼마입니까?

O : Oh, not so much, but enough to teach you a lesson.
그렇게 많지는 않지만, 당신에게 경각심을 주기에 충분합니다.

미국에서 낚시를 하려면 가까운 낚시점이나 공원관리국에서 발행하는 라이선스(허가증)를 구입해야 한다. 괌, 사이판, 하와이 등 원주민들이 낚시하는 곳에서는 허가증이 필요 없지만, 미국 본토에서는 반드시 라이선스를 소지해야 한다. 라이선스는 1회용, 1년용, 민물낚시용, 바다낚시용 등 다양하게 있으니, 본인에게 필요한 것을 구입하면 된다.

부 록

Appendices

TOEIC, TOEFL, TEPS Listening Comprehension

1. 항공사 승무원
2. 관광통역 안내사
3. 호텔 서비스사
4. TEPS

TOEIC, TOEFL, TEPS Reading Comprehension

1. 관광통역 안내사
2. 호텔 서비스사
3. 항공사 승무원
4. 호텔조리사

English Sayings and Proverbs(영어 격언 및 속담)

TOEIC

TOEFL

TEPS

Listening

Comprehension

TOEIC, TOEFL, TEPS Listening Comprehension

01 항공사 승무원

▪ Listen to the conversation and choose the best answer to each question.

1. Where does this conversation take place?

   (A) Check-in counter

   (B) Reservation desk

   (C) Customs

2. How much is a business class ticket?

   (A) $610

   (B) $560

   (C) $420

3. Which class seats have been sold?

   (A) Business class

   (B) First class

   (C) Economy class

▪ Listen to the conversation and choose the best answer to each question.

Woman : A round-trip, economy class ticket to Las Vegas costs $420. Business class is $560.

Man B : What about first class?

Woman : A first class ticket costs $610, but there are no more seats available on this flight.

여자 : 라스베이거스행 왕복 일반석 항공권 요금은 420달러입니다. 비즈니스석은 560달러입니다.

남자 : 일등석은 얼마죠?

여자 : 일등석 항공권 요금은 610달러이지만, 본 항공편엔 좌석이 남은 게 없습니다.

1. Where does this conversation take place?

(A) Check-in counter

(B) Reservation desk

(C) Customs

2. How much is a business class ticket?

(A) $610

(B) $560

(C) $420

3. Which class seats have been sold?

(A) Business class

(B) First class

(C) Economy class

[정답] 1. B 2. B 3. B

▪ Listen to the short talk and choose the best answer to each question.

1. Where would one hear this announcement?

   (A) At the airport

   (B) At the bus terminal

   (C) At the train station

2. What should you do first after you arrive?

   (A) Go through customs.

   (B) Collect your luggage.

   (C) Speak to an immigration official.

- Listen to the announcement and choose the best answer to each question.

We would like to announce that Terminal Five at Jameson International Airport has made the transition from air to land even faster and more convenient than ever. Once you arrive, you will be able to go directly to one of our immigration booths. After you've spoken to one of our agents, please get a free trolley. Then, pick up your baggage from one of our high-speed carousels, and pass quickly through customs. If you have a connecting flight, you'll only be steps away from one of our fifteen departure gates. We hope these improvements will make your day a little easier.

제이미슨 국제공항의 5번 청사가 전보다 더욱 빠르고 편리하게 착륙할 수 있도록 변화되었음을 알려 드립니다. 여러분은 도착하시면 곧바로 입국심사대로 가실 수 있습니다. 저희 직원에게 말씀하신 후, 무료 짐수레를 한 대 빌려 고속 수하물용 원형 컨베이어에서 수하물을 찾으시고 세관을 신속히 통과하십시오. 접속 항공편을 이용하시는 분은 불과 몇 발자국이면 15개 탑승구 중 한 곳으로 가실 수 있게 됩니다. 저희는 이번 개선 조치로 좀 더 편안한 하루가 되시기를 바랍니다.

1. Where would one hear this announcement?

   (A) At the airport

   (B) At the bus terminal

   (C) At the train station

2. What should you do first after you arrive?

   (A) Go through customs.

   (B) Collect your luggage.

   (C) Speak to an immigration official.

[정답] 1. A 2. C

▪ Listen to the conversation and choose the best answer to each question.

1. What happened to the flight?

   (A) The flight is out of order.

   (B) The captain is waiting for a passenger.

   (C) The flight won't take off on time.

2. When will the plane be able to leave?

   (A) After 60 minutes

   (B) Before 30 minutes

   (C) After 15 minutes

3. How is the weather?

   (A) Sunny

   (B) Stormy

   (C) Cloudy

- Listen to the conversation and choose the best answer to each question.

Woman : The captain has just been informed by the control tower that our plane will be delayed in take-off.

Man A : I've never seen a storm like this. Do you have any idea how long it will take before it takes off?

Woman : They estimate at least one hour.

Man A : I'd better get some sleep.

여자 : 기장이 관제탑으로부터 비행기 출발이 지연될 거라는 연락을 방금 받았어요.
남자 : 지금껏 이런 폭풍은 본 적이 없어요. 이륙까지 시간이 얼마나 걸릴 것 같나요?
여자 : 최소한 한 시간은 걸린대요.
남자 : 잠을 좀 자는 게 낫겠군요.

1. What happened to the flight?
   (A) The flight is out of order.
   (B) The captain is waiting for a passenger.
   (C) The flight won't take off on time.

2. When will the plane be able to leave?
   (A) After 60 minutes
   (B) Before 30 minutes
   (C) After 15 minutes

3. How is the weather?
   (A) Sunny
   (B) Stormy
   (C) Cloudy

[정답] 1. C 2. A 3. B

▪ Listen to the short talk and choose the best answer to each question.

1. Who is making this announcement?
   (A) Captain
   (B) Conductor
   (C) Tour guide

2. What is the port of entry?
   (A) Gimpo
   (B) Seoul
   (C) New York

▪ Listen to the conversation and choose the best answer to each question.

Good afternoon, ladies and gentleman. This is the captain. Welcome aboard flight 432 bound for Seoul. We will be cruising at a moderate altitude. Our flight time to Seoul is expected to be approximately 11 hours and we should arrive in Seoul at 6:30 local time. If you have any questions about connecting flights, please see the Northwest agents at Incheon Airport, who will make modifications to your flight. We hope you have a pleasant and enjoyable flight. Thank you.

승객 여러분, 안녕하세요. 기장입니다. 서울행 432항공편에 탑승하신 것을 환영합니다. 이 비행기는 적정 고도로 운항할 것입니다. 서울까지의 비행시간은 약 11시간으로 예상되며 현지 시각 6시 30분에 서울에 도착할 예정입니다. 접속 항공편에 의문이 있으신 분은 인천공항의 노스웨스트 직원들을 찾아가시면 비행 일정을 조정해 드릴 것입니다. 쾌적하고 즐거운 여행이 되시기를 바랍니다. 감사합니다.

1. Who is making this announcement?
   (A) Captain
   (B) Conductor
   (C) Tour guide

2. What is the port of entry?
   (A) Incheon
   (B) Seoul
   (C) New York

[정답] 1. A 2. A

TOEIC, TOEFL, TEPS Listening Comprehension

02 관광통역 안내사

▪ Listen to the conversation and choose the best answer to each question.

1. Where is the man interested to go on his vacation?

   (A) Pacific

   (B) Australia

   (C) Europe

2. What are they looking at?

   (A) A newspaper

   (B) A tour schedule

   (C) A beautiful scene

- Listen to the conversation and choose the best answer to each question.

Woman : Where are you planning to go on your vacation?

Man A : Australia and New Zealand. Fortunately, The Pacific Travel Agency on Smith Street is promoting a special tour package for the two countries.

Woman : I've always wanted to go there.

Man A : Me too! Look at this itinerary! The tour is full of sightseeing. Also, the accommodations appear to have a four-star rating.

여자 : 휴가 동안 어디에 가실 계획인가요?

남자 : 호주와 뉴질랜드요. 마침 스미스가의 퍼시픽 여행사에서 두 나라로 가는 특선 투어패키지를 홍보 중이에요.

여자 : 늘 거기에 가고 싶었는데.

남자 : 나도 그랬어요! 이 여행 일정을 봐요! 투어가 볼거리로 가득해요. 또, 숙박시설은 별 4개짜리 등급인 것 같아요.

1. Where is the man interested to go on his vacation?

(A) Pacific

(B) Australia

(C) Europe

2. What are they looking at?

(A) A newspaper

(B) A tour schedule

(C) A beautiful scene

[정답] 1. B 2. B

▪ Listen to the short talk and choose the best answer to each question.

1. Who is this advertisement aimed at?
   (A) The general public
   (B) Travel agents
   (C) Newspaper readers

2. How much can you save on the tour that stops in Prague?
   (A) $350
   (B) $500
   (C) $700

3. Who decides when the travel dates will be?
   (A) The airlines
   (B) Customers
   (C) The travel agency

▪ Listen to the announcement and choose the best answer to each question.

All Sunday Travel readers can take advantage of exclusive savings between ten percent and twenty percent on a wide range of holidays for the coming year if they book before December 31st. If you choose Eastern Europe, you could save $350 on a 15-day journey for two through Vienna, Prague, Budapest and Istanbul. Or, you could choose an 18-day journey to Rumania. Our United Travelers packages contain a wide selection of multi-holidays, cruise and fly-drive tours. Dates are determined by Bates Travel.

선데이 트래블의 모든 독자 여러분은 12월 31일 이전까지 예약하실 경우 내년 광범위한 휴가 경비의 10~20% 특별 할인 혜택을 받을 수 있습니다. 만일 여러분이 동유럽을 선택하신다면 여러분은 비엔나, 프라하, 부다페스트, 그리고 이스탄불을 경유하는 15일짜리 2인용 여행에서 350달러를 절약할 수 있습니다. 그렇지 않으면 루마니아로 가는 18일 여행을 선택할 수도 있습니다. 우리 유나이티드 트래블러서의 패키지에는 선택의 폭이 넓은 다양한 휴일 상품, 선박 여행과 육항로 투어 상품이 있습니다. 날짜는 베이츠 여행사가 결정합니다.

1. Who is this advertisement aimed at?
   (A) The general public (B) Travel agents
   (C) Newspaper readers

2. How much can you save on the tour that stops in Prague?
   (A) $350 (B) $500 (C) $700

3. Who decides when the travel dates will be?
   (A) The airlines (B) Customers
   (C) The travel agency

[정답] 1. C 2. A 3. C

▪ Listen to the conversation and choose the best answer to each question.

1. Which vehicle will the man use to get to work?
    (A) A car
    (B) A train
    (C) A bus

2. What is true about Highway 7?
    (A) There was a car accident.
    (B) It is under construction.
    (C) There is protest.

3. Which way should you take if you drive to work?
    (A) Any roads but Highway 7
    (B) The crosswalks
    (C) Highway 7

▪ Listen to the conversation and choose the best answer to each question.

Man B : I usually drive to work, but today I decided to commute by train since the traffic has been congested lately.

Woman : I know what you mean. Highway 7 is under construction, so all the vehicles have to make a detour.

Man B : Many cars couldn' t help being stuck in traffic jams.

Woman : My friend told me several intersections were blocked. Pedestrians had to make their way around the cars__they were literally blocking the crosswalks.

남자 : 대개 차를 갖고 출근하지만, 요즘 교통이 혼잡해서 오늘은 기차로 통근하기로 했어요.

여자 : 무슨 뜻인지 알겠어요. 7번 고속도로가 공사 중이라 모든 차량이 돌아서 가야 하죠.

남자 : 많은 차들이 교통 체증에 갇힐 수밖에 없었죠.

여자 : 친구는 몇 군데 교차로가 막혀서 행인들이 차들 사이로 빠져나가야 했다더군요—말 그대로 차들이 횡단보도를 막았던 거죠

1. Which vehicle will the man use to get to work?

(A) A car (B) A train (C) A bus

2. What is true about Highway 7?

(A) There was a car accident. (B) It is under construction.

(C) There is a protest.

3. Which way should you take if you drive to work?

(A) Any roads but Highway 7 (B) The crosswalks

(C) Highway 7

[정답] 1. B 2. B 3. A

▪ Listen to the short talk and choose the best answer to each question.

1. What is this speaker's job?

   (A) Traffic reporter

   (B) Police officer

   (C) Bus driver

2. How will the traffic condition be?

   (A) Light

   (B) Medium

   (C) Heavy

3. What does the speaker suggest you do if you want to drive past 42nd street?

   (A) Take a bus

   (B) Drive right through the area

   (C) Avoid the whole area

▪ Listen to the announcement and choose the best answer to each question.

Today is going to be a big traffic day. There is a large gathering of foreign officials at the United Nations, and the traffic in midtown, in fact throughout Manhattan, will be a mess. Here's the story as we know it now : 42nd street will be closed from 1st Avenue to Park Avenue. And 1st Avenue will be closed from 39th to 45th street. If you are planning to drive through this area, I'd suggest you make a wide circle around this entire area.

오늘은 교통이 매우 혼잡하겠습니다. 국제 연합에서 열리는 외국 관리들의 대규모 회의 때문에 시내 중심부, 즉 맨해튼 전 지역에 걸쳐 혼잡이 예상됩니다. 현재 진행 상황은 다음과 같습니다. 42번가는 1번에서 파크로까지 폐쇄될 것입니다. 그리고 1번로는 39번가에서 45번가까지 폐쇄되겠습니다. 이 지역을 차를 갖고 지나시려는 분은 이 지역전체를 크게 돌아가는 것이 좋겠습니다.

1. What is this speaker's job?
   (A) Traffic reporter (B) Police officer
   (C) Bus driver

2. How will the traffic conditions be?
   (A) Light (B) Medium (C) Heavy

3. What does the speaker suggest you do if you want to drive past 42nd street?
   (A) Take a bus
   (B) Drive right through the area
   (C) Avoid the whole area

[정답] 1. A 2. C 3. C

▪ Listen to the conversation and choose the best answer to each question.

1. Who does the man want to speak to?

   (A) Mr. James

   (B) Mr. Mars

   (C) Mr. Roy

2. What is Mr. James doing now?

   (A) He is having a conference.

   (B) He is on the line.

   (C) He is meeting one of his clients.

▪ Listen to the conversation and choose the best answer to each question.

Woman : Good afternoon, Gilbert and Roy. This is Wanda. How can I help you?

Man B : I' m trying to get in touch with Mr. James. Is he in?

Woman : Sorry. He' s in a meeting with a client right now. Would you like to leave a message?

Man B : Yes, my name is Texe Marrs. Please tell him to call me when he' s free. I am in my office right now.

여자 : 안녕하세요. 길버트 앤 로이의 완다입니다. 무엇을 도와드릴까요?

남자 : 제임스씨와 통화하려고요. 지금 계신가요?

여자 : 죄송하지만 지금 고객과 상담 중인데요. 메시지를 남기시겠어요?

남자 : 네, 이름은 텍스마스고요. 시간 있을 때 전화해달라고 전해주세요. 지금 내 사무실에 있어요.

1. Who does the man want to speak to?

(A) Mr. James

(B) Mr. Marrs

(C) Mr. Roy

2. What is Mr. James doing now?

(A) He is having a conference.

(B) He is on the line.

(C) He is meeting one of his clients.

[정답] 1. A 2. C

▪ Listen to the short talk and choose the best answer to each question.

1. When can you save money on calls throughout North America?

(A) All day, all night

(B) Before December 31st

(C) Monday to Friday

2. How much can one save on calls within the country on weekdays?

(A) Ten percent

(B) Fifteen percent

(C) Twenty percent

3. Who will receive forty dollars worth of free calls?

(A) Company employee

(B) Country club members

(C) Anyone who joins now

▪ Listen to the advertisement and choose the best answer to each question.

Dial 1503 offers you big savings on your calls compared to basic rates of other companies. For all calls in North America, you will save fifteen percent at all times. For all national calls, you will save twenty percent Monday to Friday, and ten percent on weekends. At all times, you will save twenty-five percent on all international calls. If you join now, you can save fifty percent on calls to Europe before December 31st. In addition, you will save twenty percent on national calls, and you will receive forty dollars worth of free calls.

다이얼 1503은 타사의 기본요금 대비 통화료를 대폭 절약해드립니다. 북미의 모든 통화의 경우, 항상 15퍼센트가 절약됩니다. 국내의 모든 통화의 경우, 평일에는 20퍼센트, 주말에는 10퍼센트가 절약됩니다. 언제든지 모든 국제 전화는 25퍼센트가 절약됩니다. 만일 여러분이 지금 가입하시면 12월 31일 이전의 유럽으로의 통화는 50퍼센트를 절약하실 수 있습니다. 추가로, 국내 통화에서 20퍼센트를 절약하시게 되고, 40달러 상당의 무료 통화 혜택을 받으시게 됩니다.

1. When can you save money on calls throughout North America?

(A) All day, all night (B) Before December 31st

(C) Monday to Friday

2. How much can one save on calls within the country on weekdays?

(A) Ten percent (B) Fifteen percent

(C) Twenty percent

3. Who will receive forty dollars worth of free calls?

(A) Company employee (B) Country club members

(C) Anyone who joins now

[정답] 1. A 2. C 3. C

▪ Listen to the conversation and choose the best answer to each question.

1. What will tomorrow's weather be like?

(A) Rain

(B) Snow

(C) Generally sunny

2. Why will the man have to check his car?

(A) They should go shopping.

(B) It will be freezing.

(C) He will leave early in the morning.

▪ Listen to the conversation and choose the best answer to each question.

Woman : Tomorrow's forecast says we may have a blizzard.
Man B : What will the temperature be?
Woman : It will be minus fifteen degrees Celsius in the early morning. So, you'd better check your van before you go shopping tomorrow.
Man B : Oh, I really hate winter!

여자 : 내일 일기 예보에는 눈보라가 있을 거래요.
남자 : 기온은 어떻대요?
여자 : 새벽엔 섭씨 영하15도가 된대요. 그러니까 내일 쇼핑을 가기 전에 당신 밴을 점검하는 게 낫겠어요.
남자 : 오, 겨울은 진짜 싫어요.

1. What will tomorrow's weather be like?
   (A) Rainy
   (B) Snowy
   (C) Generally sunny

2. Why will the man have to check his car?
   (A) They should go shopping.
   (B) It will be freezing.
   (C) He will leave early in the morning.

[정답] 1. B 2. B

▪ Listen to the short talk and choose the best answer to each question.

1. Where is it expected to snow?
   (A) In the Northeast
   (B) In the Southwest
   (C) In the Midwest

2. What is unusual about weather in the Southeast?
   (A) The heavy rain
   (B) The warm temperatures
   (C) The amount of snow

3. What is the weather like in the Northwest?
   (A) Warm and dry
   (B) Clear skies and sunshine
   (C) Periodic rain and snow

- Listen to the forecast and choose the best answer to each question.

The weather in the Northwest calls for light rain in the morning, followed by thundershowers in the afternoon.
Temperatures should be in the low 40s all day. Most of the Southeast should see clear skies and a lot of sunshine. Temperatures will reach up into the 50s. This is highly unusual for this time of year. By contrast, the Midwest will be hit with unusually cold temperatures and winter-like conditions. In fact, there is a snow advisory for both St. Louis and Kansas City. The Southwest will be dry and warm. Temperatures shouldn' t drop below 60 in most parts of Arizona and New Mexico. Weather in the Pacific Northwest calls for rain on-and-off throughout the day, with snow falling intermittently in the Cascades.

북동부의 날씨를 예보하면 아침에 약간의 비가 내리고, 이어서 오후에 뇌우가 있겠습니다. 기온은 하루 종일 40도에서 45도를 밑돌겠습니다. 남동부 대부분 지역에서는 맑은 하늘과 맑은 햇살을 보실 수 있습니다. 기온은 50도대로 오르겠습니다. 이것은 한 해의 이맘 때 기온으로는 매우 특이한 현상입니다. 대조적으로 중서부 지역은 특이하게 낮은 기온과 겨울 같은 날씨를 맞겠습니다. 사실 세인트루이스와 캔자스시에 눈이 올 예정이라는 기상특보가 들어와 있습니다. 남서부 지역은 건조하고 따뜻하겠습니다. 애리조나의 뉴멕시코 대부분 지역의 기온은 60도 아래로 떨어지지는 않겠습니다. 태평양 연안 북서부의 날씨를 보면 하루 종일 드문드문 비가 내리고, 캐스케이즈에는 가끔 눈이 내릴 것으로 예상됩니다.

1. Where is it expected to snow?

(A) In the Northeast

(B) In the Southwest

(C) In the Midwest

2. What is unusual about weather in the Southeast?

(A) The heavy rain

(B) The warm temperatures

(C) The amount of snow

3. What is the weather like in the Northwest?

(A) Warm and dry

(B) Clear skies and sunshine

(C) Periodic rain and snow

[정답] 1. C 2. B 3. C

- Listen to the conversation and choose the best answer to each question.

1. What does the woman want to send?

   (A) A postcard

   (B) A parcel

   (C) A telegram

2. How many ways can the woman send the mail?

   (A) One

   (B) Two

   (C) Three

▪ Listen to the conversation and choose the best answer to each question.

Woman : I'd like to send this parcel to Japan.
Man A : How would you like it sent?
Woman : What are the options?
Man A : You can send it by express or through regular air freight.

여자 : 일본으로 이 소포를 보내고 싶은데요.
남자 : 어떻게 보내실 겁니까?
여자 : 어떤 방법이 있나요?
남자 : 빠른우편이나 보통 항공 화물로 보낼 수 있습니다.

1. What does the woman want to send?
    (A) A postcard
    (B) A parcel
    (C) A telegram

2. How many ways can the woman send the mail?
    (A) One
    (B) Two
    (C) Three

[정답] 1. B 2. B

▪ Listen to the short talk and choose the best answer to each question.

1. How many pieces of mail did the Postal Service handle last year?
   (A) Over two million pieces
   (B) Over two billion pieces
   (C) Over two hundred thousand pieces

2. How long will it take to send a mail to Japan if there is no need to go through customs?
   (A) Three days
   (B) Four days
   (C) Five days

▪ Listen to the announcemnt and choose the best answer to each question.

Last year, the Postal Service forwarded over two billion pieces of mail. As you can imagine, it is an extremely labor-intensive and costly endeavor. We publish service standards of the normally expected time of delivery as a guide for our customers. In most cases, if it does not have to go through customs, it will be delivered in 2 days to Canada and major European countries. Delivery to the Pacific Rim countries and other destinations generally takes 3 days. If an item must go through customs in the designated country, one day should normally be added to the delivery time to allow for customs clearance.

지난해에 우편국은 20억 통 이상의 우편물을 발송했습니다. 여러분이 짐작하시는 대로 이것은 극히 노동집약적이고 고비용이 드는 힘든 작업입니다. 저희는 고객 여러분을 위한 안내서로서 정상적으로 예상되는 배달 소요시간의 기준 표를 발행했습니다. 대부분의 경우, 세관을 통과할 필요가 없는 우편물은 이틀이면 캐나다와 주요 유럽국가로 배달될 것입니다. 태평양 연안 국가와 기타 목적지로의 배달은 일반적으로 3일이 걸리게 됩니다. 만일 우편물이 해당 국가의 세관을 통과해야 한다면 통관을 위해 보통 하루가 더 걸립니다.

1. How many pieces of mail did the Postal Service handle last year?
   (A) Over two million pieces (B) Over two billion pieces
   (C) Over two hundred thousand pieces

2. How long will it take to send mail to Japan if there is no need to go through customs?
   (A) Three days (B) Four days
   (C) Five days

[정답] 1. B 2. A

▪ Listen to the conversation and choose the best answer to each question.

1. Where did the car break down?

   (A) At a parking lot

   (B) In the woman's garage

   (C) At an intersection

2. What kind of a car does she have?

   (A) A very expensive car

   (B) A second-hand car

   (C) A compact car

▪ Listen to the conversation and choose the best answer to each question.

Woman : I tried to start my luxury car this morning, but failed.
Man B : Where did that happen?
Woman : In my garage at home.
Man B : You were very fortunate to have that happen near your house.

여자 : 오늘 아침에 내 고급 차에 시동을 걸려고 했지만 실패했어요.
남자 : 어디서 그랬어요?
여자 : 우리 집 차고에서요.
남자 : 집 근처에서 그런 일이 생긴 게 천만 다행이군요.

1. Where did the car break down?

(A) At a parking lot

(B) In the woman's garage

(C) At an intersection

2. What kind of a car does she have?

(A) A very expensive car

(B) A second-hand car

(C) A compact car

[정답] 1. B 2. A

- Listen to the short talk and choose the best answer to each question.

1. What is EVPLUS?

   (A) A car maker

   (B) A car

   (C) A salesman

2. When will CRV be able to make a profit?

   (A) Two years later

   (B) Three years later

   (C) No one knows for sure.

▪ Listen to the announcement and choose the best answer to each question.

CRV has joined the growing list of electric car makers after unveiling its EVPLUS. CRV's EVPLUS will go head-to-head with General Motor's EVI. CRV officials said it would lease 500 of the vehicles over the next three years as the first step toward gauging consumer interest in environmentally-friendly cars. However, CRV officials acknowledged the company would lose money on every electric car it sells until production volumes increase to around 400,000 cars per year.

CRV는 EVPLUS를 발표하면서 증가일로에 있는 전기차 제조업체 대열에 참여했습니다. CRV의 EVPLUS는 제너럴 모터스의 EVI와 대접전을 벌이게 될 것입니다. CRV의 관계자들은 앞으로 3년 동안 환경 친화적인 차에 대한 소비자 관심도를 측정하기 위한 첫 단계로 본 차량 500대를 임대할 것이라고 말했습니다. 하지만 CRV관계자들은 생산 규모가 연간 40만 대 정도로 증가할 때까지는, 판매하는 모든 전기차에서 손해를 보게 된다는 점을 인정했습니다.

1. What is EVPLUS?

(A) A car maker

(B) A car

(C) A salesman

2. When will CRV be able to make a profit?

(A) Two years later

(B) Three years later

(C) No one knows for sure.

[정답] 1. B 2. C

▪ Listen to the conversation and choose the best answer to each question.

1. What does the man hate doing?

   (A) Paying high prices for goods

   (B) Shopping at outlet stores

   (C) Paying wholesale prices

2. Where is the woman going to buy grocery?

   (A) Retailer

   (B) Wholesale club

   (C) Supermarket

▪ Listen to the conversation and choose the best answer to each question.

Woman : I really hate buying things at full retail.
Man B : Me, too. That's why I shop at outlet stores.
Woman : That's a good idea. Why didn't I think of that?

여자 : 난 소매가격을 다 주고 물건을 사는 게 정말 싫어요.
남자 : 나도요. 그래서 나는 할인 매장에서 쇼핑을 해요.
여자 : 그거 좋은 생각이네요. 왜 진작 그 생각을 못 했을까?

1. What does the man hate doing?
   (A) Paying high prices for goods
   (B) Shopping at outlet stores
   (C) Paying wholesale prices

2. Where is the woman going to buy her groceries?
   (A) Retailer
   (B) Wholesale club
   (C) Supermarket

[정답] 1. A 2. B

- Listen to the short talk and choose the best answer to each question.

1. Why is the department store going to have a sale?
   (A) They are celebration forty years in business.
   (B) They are relocating.
   (C) They are going out of business.

2. How many years has the company been in business?
   (A) Forty
   (B) Fifty
   (C) Sixty

3. What will not be available for sale?
   (A) Blouse
   (B) Table
   (C) Camera

▪ Listen to the announcement and choose the best answer to each question.

Macy' s department store is having a huge sale this Saturday. We will be closing our doors after forty years in business. All items in the store will be going for 50, 60 and even 70 percent off their sticker prices. Everything from clothes, household furnishings, garden tools, and even books will be included in this sale. So, come on down! We will be open from 8 a.m. to 10 p.m. Make no mistake. This will be the last day we' ll be open to the public.

메이시스 백화점이 이번 주 토요일에 엄청난 세일을 합니다. 저희는 40년 간의 영업을 끝내고 문을 닫게 됩니다. 매장의 모든 품목이 표시가의 50, 60 심지어 70%까지 할인 판매됩니다. 의류, 가정용 가구, 원예 도구부터, 심지어 책까지 모든 것을 세일합니다. 그러니까, 어서 오세요! 영업시간은 오전 8시부터 오후 10시까지입니다. 절대 놓치지 마세요. 이날이 저희가 여러분 앞에 문을 여는 마지막 날이 될 것입니다.

1. Why is the department store going to have a sale?
   (A) They are celebrating forty years in business.
   (B) They are relocating.
   (C) They are going out of business.

2. How many years has the company been in business?
   (A) Forty (B) Fifty (C) Sixty

3. What will not be available for sale?
   (A) Blouses (B) Tables (C) Cameras

[정답] 1. C 2. A 3. C

TOEIC, TOEFL, TEPS Listening Comprehension

03 호텔 서비스사

▪ Listen to the conversation and choose the best answer to each question.

1. Where is the conversation taking place?

   (A) In the Airport

   (B) At the shop

   (C) In the hotel

2. Who might the woman be?

   (A) An operator

   (B) A receptionist

   (C) An investigator

▪ Listen to the conversation and choose the best answer to each question.

Woman : Is your personal information still the same since you last stayed with us?

Man B : Yes. Nothing has changed.

Woman : Very good. Your room number is 205.

Man B : By the way, I need a wake-up call at 6:30 every morning. And, please arrange room service for me immediately. Soup and a sandwich will be OK. As a matter of fact, I'm starving to death.

여자 : 신상 정보가 지난번 묵으실 때와 같나요?

남자 : 네, 바뀐 게 없어요.

여자 : 좋습니다. 손님 객실 번호는 205호입니다.

남자 : 그런데요. 매일 아침 6시 30분에 모닝콜이 필요합니다. 그리고 룸서비스를 즉시 준비해 주세요. 수프와 샌드위치면 돼요. 사실, 배가 고파 죽을 지경이에요.

1. Where is the conversation taking place?

(A) In the Airport

(B) At the shop

(C) In the hotel

2. Who might the woman be?

(A) An operator

(B) A receptionist

(C) An investigator

[정답] 1. C 2. B

- Listen to the short talk and choose the best answer to each question.

1. What is the main subject of this talk?
   (A) Wall Street
   (B) The Star Hotel
   (C) New York city

2. Where do you NOT have easy access to?
   (A) The Statue of Liberty
   (B) Metropolitan Museum of Art
   (C) Empire State Building

3. How many cinemas does the star Star Hotel have?
   (A) Three
   (B) Four
   (C) Two

- Listen to the advertisement and choose the best answer to each question.

You can do business more efficiently when you stay at the Star Hotel. Our luxury, five-star tower is conveniently located in the heart of New York City. You' ll have an easy time of getting to Wall Street, Central Park and Soho.
In fact, we' re just minutes away from several major tourist attractions, including the Empire State Building and the Metropolitan Museum of Art. We are also within walking distance of three major shopping areas. The hotel itself has eight restaurants, four cinemas, three nightclubs, and two karaoke bars. The more you know the Big Apple, the more you' ll want to stay at New York' s finest hotel.

여러분이 스타 호텔에 머무르시면 비즈니스를 더욱 효과적으로 하실 수 있습니다. 저희의 별 다섯 개짜리 고급 호텔은 뉴욕시 중심부의 편리한 위치에 있습니다. 여러분은 월스트리트와 센트럴 파크, 소호로 쉽게 가실 수 있습니다. 사실, 저희 호텔은 엠파이어 스테이트 빌딩, 메트로폴리탄 미술관을 포함한 몇몇 주요 관광 명소들로부터 몇 분 거리에 있습니다. 저희는 또한 세 개의 주요 쇼핑 구역에 걸어서 갈 수 있는 거리에 위치하고 있습니다. 호텔자체에 여덟 곳의 레스토랑과 네 곳의 극장, 세 곳의 나이트클럽, 그리고 두 곳의 가라오케 바가 있습니다. 여러분이 빅 애플을 알면 알수록 뉴욕에서 가장 멋진 호텔에서 머물고 싶어질 겁니다.

1. What is the main subject of this talk?

   (A) Wall Street

   (B) The Star Hotel

   (C) New York city

2. Where do you NOT have easy access to?

   (A) The Statue of Liberty

   (B) Metropolitan Museum of Art

   (C) Empire State Building

3. How many cinemas does the Star Hotel have?

   (A) Three

   (B) Four

   (C) Two

[정답] 1. B 2. A 3. B

▪ Listen to the conversation and choose the best answer to each question.

1. What are they doing?
   (A) Ordering some more wine
   (B) Choosing a wine to drink
   (C) Complaining about the meal

2. What is the chardonnay?
   (A) A name of a wine
   (B) The waiter' s name
   (C) The woman' s nickname

3. What is the woman going to do?
   (A) She will call a waiter.
   (B) She will order some South African wine.
   (C) She will go to the counter.

▪ Listen to the conversation and choose the best answer to each question.

Man A : Did you find any special wine you want to drink?
Woman : There appear to be some good South African wine bottles there.
Man A : This chardonnay might be worth trying.
Woman : Let's try it then. I'll get the waiter's attention so we can order.

남자 : 특별히 마시고 싶은 와인을 찾았나요?
여자 : 저기 좋은 남아프리카 와인 병들이 있는 것 같은데요.
남자 : 이 샤도네가 마셔볼 만하겠군요.
여자 : 그러면 어디 마셔봅시다. 주문하게 웨이터를 부를게요.

1. What are they doing?

(A) Ordering some more wine
(B) Choosing a wine to drink
(C) Complaining about the meal

2. What is the chardonnay?

(A) A name of a wine
(B) The waiter's name
(C) The woman's nickname

3. What is the woman going to do?

(A) She will call a waiter.
(B) She will order some South African wine.
(C) She will go to the counter.

[정답] 1. B 2. A 3. A

▪ Listen to the short talk and choose the best answer to each question.

1. What is the focus of this talk?
   (A) A store
   (B) A restaurant
   (C) A hotel

2. What day is Jake's closed?
   (A) Saturday
   (B) Sunday
   (C) Monday

3. What does the speaker recommend you to do?
   (A) Stop by for lunch sometime.
   (B) Try some of the seafood.
   (C) Make reservations for a table.

II. Listen to the conversation and choose the best answer to each question.

At Jack's, we've been serving the best seafood in town for over a hundred years. The minute you walk in the door you will sense the tradition. More importantly, you will know you're in for a fine dining experience. We are open Tuesday to Friday from 10 a.m. to 2 p.m. for lunch, and 5 p.m. to 10 p.m. for dinner. On Saturday and Sunday we are only open from 6 p.m. to 10 p.m.
Reservations are not necessary, but we strongly encourage you to call ahead as there is limited seating available.

저희 제이크스 레스토랑에서는 100년이 넘게 시내에서 최고의 해물요리를 접대해 왔습니다. 여러분이 문을 들어서는 순간 전통을 느끼게 될 것입니다. 더 중요한 것은 멋진 만찬을 경험하게 됐다고 깨닫게 될 거라는 점입니다. 화요일에서 금요일까지의 저희 영업시간은 점심식사는 오전 10시에서 오후 2시까지, 저녁식사는 오후 6시부터 10시까지입니다. 토요일과 일요일은 오후 6시에서 10시까지만 영업합니다. 예약하실 필요는 없지만 좌석이 한정된 관계로 사전에 전화 주시기를 권하는 바입니다.

1. What is the focus of this talk?

(A) A store (B) A restaurant (C) A hotel

2. What day is Jake's closed?

(A) Saturday (B) Sunday (C) Monday

3. What does the speaker recommend you to do?

(A) Stop by for lunch sometime.
(B) Try some of the seafood.
(C) Make reservations for a table.

[정답] 1. B 2. C 3. C

TOEIC, TOEFL, TEPS Listening Comprehension

04 TEPS

1. W : How do you spell your name?

   M : ______________________ .

   (a) My name's Gary Park.
   (b) I'm Gary.
   (c) G–A–R–Y.
   (d) May I have your name?

W : 당신의 이름은 철자가 어떻게 되십니까? M : G–A–R–Y (C)

2. M : I've heard you are good at computers and English.

   W : I heard the same about you. How's your company's business?

   M : It's doing well. What's your position in your company?

   W : ______________________ .

   (a) I'm working on the 7th floor.
   (b) I assist the president of the company.
   (c) I got a raise last month.
   (d) Sometimes the modem of my computer doesn't work.

M : 컴퓨터와 영어를 잘한다고 들었습니다. W : 당신도 잘한다는 소릴 들었어요. 사업은 어떻게 되갑니까? M : 잘 되고 있어요. 회사에서 직급이 어떻게 됩니까? W : 저는 사장의 비서로 있습니다. (b)

3. W : How do you do? I'm Grace.

   M : I'm very glad to meet you, Grace. I'm Danny.

   W : I've heard a lot about you from Ann. By the way, congratulations! When are you and Ann going to marry?

W : 처음 뵙겠습니다. 저는 그레이스라고 합니다. M : 만나 뵙게 되어 반갑습니다, 그레이스. 저는 대니라고 합니다. W : 앤으로부터 이야기 많이 들었습니다. 그나저나 축하드립니다. 앤과는 언제 결혼합니까?

M : 아마 오는 10월쯤 에요. 그런데 저는 우선 직장을 구해야 해요.
W : 빠른 시간 내에 좋은 직장을 구하시기를 바랍니다. 대학때 전공은 무엇이었죠?
M : 앤과 같습니다. 회계학을 전공했어요.
W : 은행에 지원해 보시지 않으셨나요?
M : 아뇨, 지원했어요, 어제 면접을 보고 결과를 기다리고 있습니다.
W : 행운을 빕니다.

Q . 대화에 따르면, 남자는 무엇을 가장 걱정하는가?

(d)

M : Maybe this coming October. But I have to find a job first.
W : I hope you find a good job soon. What was your major in college?
M : The same as Ann's. We majored in accounting.
W : Didn't you apply to any banks?
M : Yes, I did. I'd an interview yesterday and I'm waiting for the result.
W : Good luck to you.

Q According to the conversation, what is the man most concerned about?

(a) Taking out a bank loan.
(b) Relaxing and sleeping.
(c) Changing jobs.
(d) Getting a job.

신입 사원을 소개하겠습니다. 이분은 지난주에 우리 회사에 입사했습니다. 27세이고 대학에서 컴퓨터 공학을 전공했습니다. 석사 과정에 입학하는 대신에 우리 회사에 지원하였습니다. 컴퓨터뿐만이 아니라 영어도 잘합니다. 따라서 컴퓨터 프로그래밍 작업 및 캐나다 지사와의 기술 제휴 적임자라고 생각됩니다. 간단히 말해서 이 사원은 아주 유망합니다. 당분간은 우리 연구개발부에서 일하게 될 것입니다. 질문이 있으시면 서슴지 말고 그에게 질문해 주십시오.

4. Let me introduce a new employee. He joined our company last week. He's 27 years old and majored in computer science at college. Instead of going for his master's degree, he applied to work for our company. He's good at English as well as computers. So he is thought to be suited for computer programming and also for technical cooperation with our branch office in Canada. In short, he is very promising. For now, he will work in our department for research and development. If you have any questions, feel free to ask him.

Q Which of the following best describes the main purpose of the passage?

(a) To introduce a new employee and his job.
(b) To provide reasons why we should learn about computers.
(c) To call on the employees to develop their abilities more.
(d) To persuade new employees to continue studying.

다음 중 위 글의 요지를 가장 잘 묘사하고 있는 것은 어느 것인가?

(a)

5. W : Hello. This is Ann. May I speak to Ted?
M : ____________________ .

(a) I' d like to make a call to Ted.
(b) Hold on, please.
(c) Hang up the phone, please.
(d) I' ll put you through to Dr. Jackson.

W : 여보세요, 앤인데요 테드 좀 바꿔주시겠어요?
M : 기다리세요.

(b)

6. W : Operator. May I help you?
M : I'd like to make a collect call to New York City.
W : What number are you going to call?
M : ______________________ .

(a) It' s a good number to memorize.
(b) I' ll call the operator immediately.
(c) Check the telephone directory, please.
(d) The area code is 212, and the phone number is 255-2501.

W : 교환입니다. 어떻게 도와드릴까요?
M : 뉴욕으로 수신자 부담 전화를 걸고 싶습니다.
W : 몇 번에 거시겠습니까?
M : 지역번호 212, 전화번호 255국의 2501번입니다.

(d)

7. W : Good morning. Mr. Kelly's office.
M : May I take with Mr. Kelly, please?
W : I'm sorry, he's on another line. May I ask who's calling?
M : This is Mr. Gregory.
W : Mr. Gregory, may I have him call you back?
M : Yes, please ask him to return my call.
W : Does he have your phone number?
M : Yes, he does.

Q What can be inferred from the dialogue?

(a) Mr. Kelly doesn't want to see Mr. Gregory.
(b) The woman doesn't want to see Mr. Gregory.
(c) Mr. Kelly will call Mr. Gregory.
(d) Tomorrow they will get together for dinner.

W : 안녕하세요. 켈리 씨 사무실입니다.
M : 켈리 씨와 통화할 수 있습니까?
W : 죄송합니다만 통화중인데요, 누구 신지 여쭤봐도 될까요?
M : 저는 그레고리라고 합니다.
W : 전화하라고 전해 드릴까요? 그레고리씨?
M : 예. 제게 전화해 달라고 전해 주세요.
W : 당신의 전화번호를 알고 계신가요?
M : 예. 그렇습니다.

대화로부터 알 수 있는 것은 무엇인가?
(c)

8. Hello. You've reached 916-3546. I'm not in at the moment, but if you want to leave a message, please wait for the beep, then speak. To send a fax, press 3 on your telephone, and hold the button down for five seconds. As soon as you hear a steady tone, press the start button on your fax machine.

Q Which of the following is true according to the passage?

안녕하세요. 당신이 전화 거신 곳은 916-3546번입니다. 저는 지금 부재중입니다. 메모를 남기시려면 삐 소리가 나기를 기다렸다가 말씀해 주세요. 팩스를 보내시려면 전화기의 3번 버튼을 5초간 계속 누르고 계십시오. 연속음이 들리면 팩스의 시작 버튼을 누르십시오.

위 글에 따르면 다음 중 어느 것이 옳은가?
(a)

(a) The speaker is explaining how to send a message to him.
(b) The speaker bought a fax machine a couple of days ago.
(c) To send a fax, press 5 for three seconds.
(d) With this fax, there is no need to push the start button.

9. M : I'd like to buy this green bag. How bmuch does it cost?
W : ______________________.

(a) You' d better take the green one.
(b) The blue bag is cheaper than the green one.
(c) The blue bag is the cheapest.
(d) Those green ones are $20 each.

M : 이 녹색 가방을 사려고 하는데, 가격이 얼마입니까?
W : 그 녹색 가방은 하나에 20달러입니다.

(d)

10. M : How much is this shirt?
W : It's 27 dollars and 99 cents.
M : May I try it on?
W : ____________.

(a) We' re all sold out.
(b) Sorry, but we don' t want it.
(c) Sure. The fitting room' s over there.
(d) We' ve discounted 5% off the regular price.

M : 이 셔츠는 얼마죠?
W : 27달러 99센트입니다.
M : 입어봐도 될까요?
W : 물론이죠. 탈의실은 저쪽에 있습니다.

(c)

11. W : May I help you?
M : Yes, I'd like to buy a birthday gift for my father. I'm looking for a shirt.

W : 무엇을 도와 드릴까요?
M : 예. 아버지 생일 선물을 사고 싶습니다. 셔츠를 찾고 있어요.

W : 이건 어떻습니까? 세일해서 19달러 99센트입니다.
M : 좋아 보이네요. 좋아요. 그걸로 사겠습니다.
W : 어떻게 지불하시겠습니까? 현금 혹은 수표?
M : 비자카드를 받습니까?
W : 예, 받습니다. 저희는 비자, 마스터, 아메리칸 익스프레스 카드를 받습니다.
M : 알겠습니다. 비자카드로 지불하겠습니다.

대화로부터 알 수 있는 것은 무엇인가?

(d)

W : How about this one? It's on sale for only nineteen dollars and ninety-nine cents.
M : That looks good. Ok, I'll take it.
W : How would you like to pay, cash or check?
M : Do you accept Visa card?
W : Yes we do. We accept Visa. Master and American Express cards.
M : OK. I'll pay by Visa.

Q Which can be known from the dialogue?

(a) The man tried on a shirt at the clothing store.
(b) The man tried on a shirt at the clothing store
(c) The woman didn't have any shirts.
(d) The man will buy a shirt by credit card.

손님 여러분께 알려 드립니다. 지금 시각이 4시 15분입니다. 저희 대학 서점은 15분 후에 영업을 마칩니다. (구입하실 책에 대한) 최종 선택을 내리신 후 계산대로 가주시기 바랍니다. 저희 서점의 영업 시간은 평일에는 오전 8시에서부터 오후 4시 30분까지이고, 토요일에는 오전 10시부터 오후 4시까지이며, 일요일에는 휴점합니다. 이번 주말이 공휴일인 관계로 이번 금요일만 정오에 문을 닫습니다. 저희 서점을 이용해 주셔서 감사합니다.

이번 금요일에 이 서점은 언제 문을 닫는가?

(a)

12. Attention. shoppers.! It is now a quarter past four. This University Bookstore will close in fifteen minutes. Please make your final selections and proceed to the check-out counters. The bookstore is open from 8:00a.m. to 4:30p.m. on weekdays, 10:00a.m. to 4:00p.m on Saturdays. It is closed on Sundays. This Friday only, we will close at noon due to the holiday weekend. Thank you for shopping with us.

Q When will the bookstore close this Friday?

(a) 12:00 p.m. (b) 3:00 p.m.
(c) 4:00 p.m. (d) 4:30 p.m.

13. M : What would you like for lunch?
W : ________________ .

(a) It was very delicious.
(b) I was starving to death.
(c) I enjoyed it very much.
(d) I' d like a hamburger and fries.

M : 점심에 무엇을 먹고 싶습니까?
W : 햄버거와 감자 튀김을 먹고 싶습니다.

(d)

14. M : Waitress!
W : Can I get you anything else?
M : No, thanks. We' ve enjoyed our meal. Bring me the check, please.
W :____________________ .

(a) Good night. Thank you for coming.
(b) We don' t accept personal checks.
(c) OK, I' ll be right back with it.
(d) Here is the menu, sir.

M : 여기요!
W : 뭐 다른 걸 더 가져다 드릴까요?
M : 아니, 됐습니다. 식사를 잘 했습니다. 계산서 좀 갖다 주세요.
W : 알겠습니다. 금방 갖다 드리겠습니다.

(c)

15. W : Are you ready to order?
M : Do you have a special for today?
W : Yes, we do. It' s a sirloin steak served with mixed salad.
M : Sounds good! Let me try it.
W : How would you like your steak?
M : Medium rare, please.
W : What kind of dressing would you like?
M : I' d like French dressing

Q What is the probable relationship between the two speakers?

(a) Driver and passenger.

W : 주문하시겠습니까?
M : 오늘의 특별 요리가 있나요?
W : 예, 있습니다. 혼합 샐러드를 곁들인 등심 스테이크입니다.
M : 괜찮을 것 같군요! 그걸 먹겠습니다.
W : 스테이크는 어떻게 해 드릴까요?
M : 약간만 덜 구어 주세요.
W : 드레싱은 어떤 걸로 드릴까요?
M : 프렌치 샐러드로 주세요.

두 명의 화자는 어떤 관계인가?

(c)

(b) Neighbor and neighbor.
(c) Waitress and customer.
(d) Butcher and customer.

16. The terminal cafeteria is having two luncheon specials right now. A club sandwich, fries and soft drink are only $3.15. A cheeseburger, onion rings and coke are only $3.75. Both are offered at a 20% savings. We also serve a breakfast special – two eggs, bacon and toast for $2.59. A fifteen percent savings. Come in and have something to eat or drink right now.

Q What is the cost of today's breakfast special?

(a) $2.20 (b) $2.59
(c) $3.15 (d) $3.75

터미널 식당에서는 지금 현재 두 종류의 점심 식사 스페셜을 판매하고 있습니다. 클럽 샌드위치, 감자 튀김, 음료수 세트는 세일하여 3달러 15센트, 치즈버거, 양파링 튀김, 콜라 세트는 3달러 75센트 입니다. 두 가지 모두 20%할인 가격에 제공되는 것입니다. 저희는 또 아침 식사 스페셜로 달걀 두 개, 베이컨, 토스트를 2달러 59센트에 제공하고 있습니다. 15% 할인 가격입니다. 어서 오셔서 음식과 음료를 드시길 바랍니다.

오늘 아침 식사 스페셜의 가격은 얼마입니까?

(b)

17. M : How far is it to the nearest drug store?
W : ______________________________ .

(a) It's open all night.
(b) You're going too far.
(c) About two hundred meters.
(d) About fifty dollars.

M : 가장 가까운 약국까지 거리가 얼마나 됩니까?
W : 약 200미터 가량 됩니다.
(c)

18. W : How are you going to the baseball stadium?
M : Can I get there by bus?
W : It's better to go by subway or by taxi.
M : ____________________ .

W : 야구장에 어떻게 갈거니?
M : 버스로 갈 수 있을까?
W : 지하철이나 택시를 타는 게 더 좋아.
M : 그러면 택시를 타겠어.
(c)

(a) OK, I'll go by bus.
(b) Maybe it'll take 30 minutes.
(c) I'll take a cab, then.
(d) Go to the football stadium instead, then.

19. W : Good afternoon! May I help you?
M : Yes, I'm looking for Mr. Randolph's office.
W : Do you have an appointment?
M : Yes, I do. I have an appointment with him at 2 o'clock.
W : Let me check... You must be Mr. Bush, right?
M : Yes, that's me.
W : All right. You go to the third floor. Go down the hall to the left. Mr. Randolph's office is the second door on your right.
M : Go down the hall to the left and the second door on my right?
W : Yes.

W : 안녕하세요! 좀 도와드릴까요?
M : 예. 저는 랜돌프 씨의 사무실을 찾고 있습니다.
W : 약속이 되어 있나요?
M : 예, 되어 있습니다. 2시에 그를 만나기로 되어 있습니다.
W : 확인해 보죠. 부시 씨 맞나요?
M : 예, 바로 접니다.
W : 알겠습니다. 3층으로 가셔서 왼쪽으로 홀을 따라 가세요. 랜돌프 씨의 사무실은 오른쪽 두 번째 방입니다.
M : 왼쪽으로 홀을 따라 가다 보면 오른쪽 두 번째 방입니까?
W : 예.

Q What will the man most likely do after the dialogue?

(a) He'll make a call to Mr. Randolph's office.
(b) He'll go to the third floor of the building.
(c) He'll go downstairs for lunch with the woman.
(d) He'll make an appointment with the woman.

대화를 마친 후 남자는 무엇을 하겠는가?

(b)

20. Attention! There is a strike going on in front of the National Assembly building. Nearly 2,000 farmers are demonstrating against the opening of the agricultural market to foreign countries. They've parked farm vehicles on the streets near the National Assembly. Traffic around the entire area is backed up. Drivers are advised not to use the roads near this area.

Q What is causing the traffic jam?

(a) Water leakage.
(b) Crops spilled on the highway.
(c) Striking bus drivers.
(d) Farmers' demonstrating.

알려드립니다. 국회 의사당 앞에서 농성이 있습니다. 2,000명에 이르는 농부들이 외국에 대한 농산물 시장 개방을 반대하며 시위를 벌이고 있습니다. 이들이 국회 부근의 도로에 농기구 차량들을 주차시켜 놓은 관계로 이 지역 전체의 교통이 정체되어 있습니다. 운전자들은 이 지역 부근의 도로를 사용하지 않기를 당부 드립니다.

교통 체증의 원인은 무엇인가?

(d)

21. M : Good morning. I'm Jay Clark, room 1050. I'm checking out now.
W : Did you enjoy your stay here?
M : Yes. Could you get my bill ready?
W : Sure. Here it is. It comes to 400 dollars. How would you like to pay?
M : I wonder if you could accept traveler's checks.
W : We accept credit cards and cash only.
M : OK. I have a Visa card.
W : Let me have it, please. (pause) Sign your name here.

Q Which of the following is true according to the dialog?

M : 안녕하세요. 저는 1050호의 제이 클라크입니다. 지금 체크아웃 하려고 하는데요.
W : 편히 지내셨습니까?
M : 예. 계산서 좀 부탁드릴까요?
W : 그러죠. 여기 있습니다. 총 400달러입니다. 어떻게 계산하시겠습니까?
M : 여행자 수표도 받나요?
W : 저희는 신용 카드와 현금만 받습니다.
M : 알겠습니다. 저한테 비자카드가 있습니다.
W : 주세요. 여기에 서명해 주시고요.

대화 내용에 비추어 볼 때 다음 중 어느 것이 옳은가?

(d)

(a) The man is checking into the hotel.
(b) The man is trying to cash a check.
(c) The woman is working at the bank.
(d) The woman works at the front desk of the hotel.

22. Attention, passengers in the terminal. Flight 207 to Miami is ready to depart from Gate 8 on the Lower Level. This is the final boarding call. Once again Flight 207 to Miami is about to depart from Gate 8 on the Lower Level. Please proceed immediately to the Gate. Flight 243 from New York will arrive at Gate 12 in just a few minutes. Flight 706 to Paris, first scheduled to leave from Gate 12, will instead depart from Gate 14. Thank you.

Q At which gate will Flight 243 from New York arrive?

(a) Gate 8. (b) Gate 12.
(c) Gate 14. (d) Gate 27.

터미널에 계신 승객 여러분께 알려 드립니다. 마이애미행 207편이 아래층8번 탑승구에서 출발할 예정입니다. 이번이 마지막 탑승 안내입니다. 다시 한 번 안내 드립니다. 마이애미행 207편이 아래층 8번 탑승구에서 출발할 예정입니다. 입구 쪽으로 바로 이동해 주시기 바랍니다. 뉴욕 발 243편은 몇 분 후 12번 탑승구로 도착할 예정입니다. 당초 12번 탑승구에서 출발하기로 예정되어 있던 파리행 706편은 12번 대신 14번 탑승구에서 출발할 예정입니다. 감사합니다.

뉴욕 발 243편은 몇 번 탑승구로 도착할 예정인가?

(b)

23. W : You ought to see a doctor about that cough right away.
M : ________________________ .

(a) I' m happy to hear from you.
(b) The doctor will prescribe medicine for you.
(c) Yes, I' m feeling much better.

W : 그런 기침은 당장 의사의 진찰을 받아 보는 게 좋겠어.
M : 그래야 할 것 같아. 며칠째 미뤄 왔지만 말야.

(d)

(d) I guess I should. I' ve been putting it off for days.

W : 안녕하세요? 오늘 어떠세요?
M : 좋아요. 고마워요. 당신은 요? 별로 좋아 보이질 않네요.
W : 예, 독감에 걸렸어요. 며칠 동안 잘 먹지를 못했어요.
M : 저런, 안 되셨네요. 빨리 낫기를 바랍니다.
(c)

24. W : Hello. How are you today?
M : I' m fine, thanks. How about you? You don' t look so good.
W : Yeah, I have a bad cold. I haven' t been eating well for days.
M : ______________________________ .

(a) You' d better turn on the air conditioner.
(b) You look pale. What' s wrong with you?
(c) That' s too bad. I hope you get well soon.
(d) Don' t worry! That' s nothing serious.

M : 지금 몇 시니? 제인?
W : 7시 55분이야. 수업 시작할 시간이 거의 다 됐어.
M : 얼마나 남았니?
W : 5분밖에 안 남았어.
(a)

25. M : What time is it, Jane?
W : It' s 7:55. It' s almost time for our class to begin.
M : How much time do we have?
W : ____________________ .

(a) We only have five minutes.
(b) It' ll take five minutes to get there.
(c) The class will be over in five minutes.
(d) I' m sorry. My watch is five minutes fast.

W : 뭘 도와 드릴까요?
M : 이 전화 이용 요청서를 다 썼어요? 그런데 궁금한 게 몇 가지 있습니다.
W : 그러세요? 뭘 알고 싶으신가요?

26. W : May I help you?
M : I filled out this request for phone service. I' ve got a couple of questions, though.
W : Sure. What do you want to know?

M : Does the monthly service charge include a telephone?

W : No, it doesn't. The charge for leasing a phone is 3 dollars per month.

M : Only 3 dollars? Okay then, I'd like to change the order to 2 phones.

W : Fine. When would you like service to start?

M : Let me see. Today is Tuesday. Can you have it done by Thursday?

W : No, I'm sorry. that takes 3 working days.

Q When can the man use the telephone service?

(a) On Tuesday. (b) On Wednesday.
(c) On Thursday. (d) On Friday.

M : 한 달 이용료에 전화기 요금도 포함되나요?

W : 아니요, 포함되지 않습니다. 전화기 한 대의 임대료는 한 달에 3달러입니다.

M : 겨우 3달러요? 좋아요. 그럼 신청 내용을 두 대로 변경하겠어요.

W : 알겠습니다. 언제부터 서비스를 받고 싶으세요?

M : 가만 보자. 오늘이 화요일이니까...목요일까지 되겠습니까?

W : 안 됩니다. 죄송하지만 설치하는 데 꼬박 사흘이 걸립니다.

남자는 전화 서비스를 언제 사용할 수 있는가?

(d)

TOEIC
TOEFL
TEPS
Reading Comprehension

TOEIC, TOEFL, TEPS Reading Comprehension

01 관광통역 안내사

■ 다음 광고를 읽고 물음에 답하시오.

Passage to India
1330 Walnut ST / 215-932-7639
Authentic Indian Cuisine served in an elegant atmosphere lunch buffet 7 days a week 11:00 to 2:30. Vegetarian $5.99 non-Vegetarian $7.99. Dinner served Sunday-Thursday 5:30 to 9:30. Friday & Saturday, 5:30 to 10:30. A live pianist on Friday & Saturday evenings. Reservations, please. Handicap accessible. Free Parking. No dress. All major cards.

Authentic Indian Cuisine(food) 전통 인도 음식
in an elegant atmosphere 우아한 분위기 속에서
7 days a week 일주일 내내 / Vegetarian 채식주의자
Reservations, please 예약필수 / Handicap accessible 장애자 이용가능
free parking 무료주차 / No dress 정장 필요 없음

인도로 가는 길
Walnut가 1330번지
전화 251-932-7639
전통 인도 요리를 우아한 분위기 속에서 매일 11시부터 2시 30분까지 점심 뷔페로 제공. 채식주의자는 5달러 99센트, 비 채식주의자는 7달러 99센트, 일요일부터 목요일까지 5시 30분부터 9시 30분까지, 금요일과 토요일은 5시 30분부터 10시 30분까지 저녁식사 제공. 금요일과 토요일 저녁에는 피아노 생음악 연주. 예약 부탁. 장애인 이용 가능. 무료 주차. 정장 필요 없음. 모든 중요 신용 카드 가능,

1. If a couple doesn't like meat, how much would they pay for lunch?

(A) $ 5.99 (B) $ 7.99

(C) $ 11.98 (D) $ 15.98

2. When is dinner available?

(A) Sunday–Thursday 5:00 to 9:00

(B) Friday 5:30 to 9:30

(C) Not available on Monday

(D) Saturday 5:30 to 10:30

3. What is NOT listed as a feature of th restaurant?

(A) Live music on weekends

(B) Cash only

(C) Reservation required

(D) Parking lot

Fall Foliage Spectacular!
Every Weekend in September!
90-minute round trips! Make it a day in the Pocono Valley at its most scenic time of year. 11:00 A.M., 1:00 P.M.,and 3:00 P.M.
Adults : $10, Seniors(55+): $9, Children(2-12) :$8, Group rates available
$1:00 OFF with this ad!
Call for Information and Reservation : 610-793-4433

fall foliage (leaves) 단풍 / round trip 왕복여행
Make it a day 하루를 즐기다 / Group rates available 단체요금 가능
$1:00 OFF with this ad(advertisement) 이 광고용지를 지참하면 1달러 할인

가을 단풍 절경!
9월은 매주 주말마다 운행!
90분간의 왕복 여행! 일년 중 가장 절경인 때 Pocono 계곡에서 하루를 즐기십시오. 오전 11시, 오후 1시 그리고 3시입니다.
성인 : 10달러, 노인(55세 이상) : 9달러, 어린이(2살에서 12살까지) : 8달러.
단체 요금도 가능합니다.
이 광고를 가져오시면 1달러를 할인해 드립니다.
안내와 예약은 610-793-4433으로 전화해 주십시오

EX

A : Why is Autumn your favorite season?
B : Because I love the cool weather and the beautiful fall ______.
(TEPS Vocab)
(a) foliage (b) vegetation
(c) verdure (d) umbrage

4. If you are sixty years old, how much should you pay without a coupon?

(A) $10.00 (B) $9.00

(C) $8.00 (D) $12.00

5. Why are the trips most popular in September?

(A) Because it is convenient everybody.

(B) Because it is most economical way.

(C) Because it is most panoramic.

(D) Because it is best time for harvest.

6. How often are the trips available daily?

(A) Three times

(B) Twice

(C) Only once in the afternoon

(D) Every hour

The Greece you've always imagined-sunny, white-washed villages, long quiet beaches, hills covered with olive trees-is the Greece you'll see with World Travel. The Greece where the ancient past exists side by side with today. In our Grecian Holiday you'll see such classical highlights as the Parthenon, the Acropolis, and Apollo's Temple, while our Athens Holiday shows you the sights, restaurants and shops of modern Athens. No other country offers so much in one vacation-natural beauty, astounding history, and a warm welcome wherever you go.

white-washed 흰색 페인트칠을 한 / covered with ~으로 덮여진
World Travel (Agency Co., Ltd.) 세계여행사 / exists side by side 공존하다
classical highlights 고전적인 명소 / a warm welcome 따뜻한 환대

세계여행사에서는 당신이 늘 꿈꿔 왔던 그리스-태양이 빛나고, 하얗게 색칠된 마을, 조용하고 긴 해변, 올리브 나무로 뒤덮인 언덕-를 보여 드리겠습니다. 그리스에는 과거의 고대와 현대가 공존하고 있습니다. 저희 아테네 할러데이 패키지에는 풍경, 식당, 상점 관광이 준비되이 있는 반면, 그리스 할러데이 패키지에는 파르테논 신전, 아크로폴리스 광장, 아폴로 신전과 같은 고대 그리스의 중요한 장소를 돌아보는 관광이 마련되어 있습니다. 어떤 나라도 한 번의 휴가에 자연경관, 놀라운 역사, 어디로 가든지 받게 되는 따뜻한 환영 등 그토록 많은 것을 보여주지는 못합니다.

7. What does this advertisement want people to do?

(A) Visit a restaurant (B) See a film
(C) Tour a foreign land (D) Take a special class

8. When would the activity take place?

(A) On a week-end (B) On a vacation
(C) One evening (D) Several evenings

Fifty percent of the households in the U.S. own a Visa Card. The nearest competitor is Master Card, with forty percent of the households. American Express has twenty percent, the now Discover Card has a close eighteen percent, and the High and Optima has one percent. When including all forms of credit cards, including those issued by department stores, better than seventy-five percent of the public use plastic.

While this may seem like a lot of credit cards, particularly considering the new tax laws that discourage credit buying, experts in the field claim the market is not yet saturated, and that there are still a lot of people who could use plastic and who do not-and the race is on to get them.

household 가족 / the nearest competitor 가장 가까운 경쟁자 – 두 번째로
those, plastic = credit cards / issued by ~가 발행한 / department store 백화점
better than = more than ~ 이상이, ~가 넘는 / this (situation) 현 상황
discourage 억제하다 / credit buying 신용카드 구매
saturated 포화된 / be on 계속되다.

미국 가정의 50%는 비자카드를 소유하고 있다. 그 다음이 마스터카드로 40%를 차지한다. 아메리칸 익스프레스는 20%, 그리고 새로 나온 디스커버카드는 18%에 가까우며, 하이 앤드 옵티마 플라스틱 조각(카드)을 사용하고 있는 셈이다. 특히 신용구매를 억제하는 새 세법을 고려할 때 현 상황은 신용카드가 너무 많은 것같이 보일지 모르나 이 분야의 전문가들은 신용카드 시장이 아직 포화상태에 달한 것은 아니라고 주장하고 있다. 이들 전문가들은 또한 플라스틱카드(신용카드)를 사용할 수 있는데도 카드를 사용하지 않는 사람들이 많아 이들을 끌기 위한 경쟁이 계속되고 있다고 주장하고 있다.

9. According to the passage, what credit card is used by more people than any other?
    (A) American Express (B) Master Card
    (C) Visa (D) Discover

10. What percent of the American public use credit cards?
    (A) Forty percent (B)Fifty percent
    (C) Seventy-five percent (D) Information not provided

11. How is credit buying treated by tax laws?
    (A) It is encouraged.
    (B) Large credit buying is discouraged, but small credit buying is encouraged.
    (C) It is not considered.
    (D) It is discouraged.

12. How do experts view the future for credit cards?
    (A) People will gradually avoid using them.
    (B) There are many people who can but do not use them.
    (C) Many people who have no credit risks hold credit cards.
    (D) It is impossible to say, because of new tax laws.

Visit Paradise Cove

For adults who wish to stay at Paradise Cove, weekly rates during the season range from $700 to $800 per person ; for children six to twelve, $600~$650. A special children's program is available for children three through five for $400 each. Children two years old and younger stay free. Rates include three family-style meals daily, and all regularly scheduled Cove activities. Rates are discounted 15% from May 21 to June 20 and 10% September 1 to 24.

If you would like to preview Paradise Cove before you make a decision to visit, a video is available free of charge by contacting the Cove at the address or phone number below. The Cove requests that you return the video when you are through with it.

weekly rates 주말요금
range from $700 to $800 per person 1인당 700에서 800달러이며
regularly scheduled Cove activities 정규 스케줄에 의한 코브 행사
make a decision 결정하다 / free of charge 무료로
be through with ~을 끝내다, ~을 다 보다

패러다이스 코브에서 묵기를 원하는 시즌 중 주당 체재비는 1인당 700-800달러이며 6세에서 12세까지의 아이들은 600달러에서 650달러이다. 3세에서 5세까지의 어린이들을 위해서는 1인당 400달러에 특별 프로그램이 마련되어 있다. 2세 이하의 어린이는 무료다. 요금에는 패밀리 스타일의 1일 3식과 정규 스케줄에 의한 모든 코브 행사들이 포함된다. 5월 21일부터 6월 20일까지는 15%, 9월 1일부터 9월 24일까지는 10%의 요금할인 혜택이 있다.

방문을 결정하기 전에 파라다이스 코브를 사전에 보기 원한다면 아래의 주소, 또는 전화로 코브에 연락하면 무료로 비디오를 빌려볼 수 있습니다. 비디오를 다 본 후에는 반환할 것을 요청합니다.

13. Using the rate schedule above, what is the least amount that two adults and three children, ages two, eight and ten, could expect to pay for the week of September 6~13 at Paradise Cove?

(A) $2,340 (B) $2,600

(C) $2,610 (D) $2,880

14. Which is true among the following statements about Paradise Cove?

(A) You receive a free video when you sign up to stay there.

(B) A three-year-old child stays for free.

(C) The Cove is open from May 21 until September 24.

(D) The Cove accepts only adult guest.

Notice to traveler :
You have purchased a non-refundable, non-transferable plane ticket good for one round-trip up to one year from the date of purchase. If any scheduling changes should be made on the coupon after reservations have been made and prior to flight, the holder will be subject to a 25% penalty on the original purchase price. Should any changes be made once flight has actually begun, there will be a 50% penalty on the remaining portion.

Notice to traveler 여행자 공지사항 / non-refundable 환불 불능의
non-transferable 양도 불능의
good for ~에 유효한 a visa good for 10 years 10년 간 유효한 비자
prior to ~에 앞서, ~ 이전에 / be subject to ~을 받다. ~을 당하다
penalty 벌금 / remaining portion 잔여금액

여행자 공지사항
귀하는 구입 일로부터 1년 동안 유효한 환불 및 양도 불능 비행기 왕복표를 구입하셨습니다. 예약 후 여행 전에 티켓에 기입한 스케줄 변경이 필요한 경우에는 고객은 원래 구입가격의 25%에 해당하는 벌금을 물게 됩니다. 일단 여행이 실제로 시작한 후에 변경을 하게 되면 잔여액의 50%를 벌금으로 물게 됩니다.

15. Which of the following statement is true?

(A) Penalties for scheduling changes prior to flight are more severe than those for changes made after one-way flight.

(B) Penalties for scheduling changes after one-way flight are more severe than for those made prior to flight.

(C) The purchased ticket is valid any time.

(D) There are no penalties assigned for scheduling changes, but reservations cannot be guaranteed.

16. What does "non-refundable, non-transferable" mean?

(A) The ticket can be used by anyone, but if unused it will not be bought back by the airline.

(B) The ticket cannot be used by another person, but if unused may be sold back to the airline at half price.

(C) If unused, the ticket will be bought back by the airline at half price, but may be used by anyone.

(D) Even if unused, the airline will not bought back the ticket and it may be used only by the person to whom it was sold.

A Review : Kilmer's Kitchen

Kilmer's Kitchen isn't very large, but the food is good. Kilmer Ragley does the cooking and his menu includes a lot of New Orleans French favorites. When I was there I had gumbo. This tasty mixture of ham and fish is cooked in a heavy pot. I thought it was delicious. For dessert I had apple surprise, a mixture of cooked apples and dough. It was too sweet for me, but you might like it if you have a taste for sweets. Kilmer has different kinds of coffee, and my espresso was a perfect end to a good dinner.

Kilmer's Kitchen, at 798 Bourbon Street, opens for dinner every evening from 5:30 to 11:00, Tuesday through Sunday. The restaurant gets very busy, so be sure to make a reservation before you go.

do the cooking 요리하다, 주방장이다 / favorites= favorite foods 특별요리, 특미
gumbo 오크라를 넣은 진한 수프 / tasty mixture 맛있는 혼합요리 / pot 냄비
dough 가루 반죽 / have a taste for ~을 좋아하다
espresso 커피의 일종, 가루를 스팀에 쐬어 진하게 만듬
perfect end to a good dinner 맛있는 저녁을 완벽하게 끝내는 후식
be sure to 틀림없이, 확실히

킬머 식당은 그리 큰 편은 아니나 음식 맛은 좋은 곳이다. 킬머 래글 리가 주방장인데 여러 가지 뉴올리언스 프랑스 특미를 메뉴로 하고 있다. 그곳에서 나는 검보 스튜를 맛보았다. 햄과 생선을 섞어 만든 이 맛있는 음식은 묵직한 냄비에 조리된다. 맛있는 것 같았다. 후식으로 조리된 사과와 빵 반죽을 섞어 만든 애플 서프라이즈를 먹었다. 내 입에는 너무 달았지만 단 것을 좋아하는 사람에게는 맛이 있을지도 모른다. 킬머 식당은 다양한 종류의 커피를 내고 있는데 에스프레소는 훌륭한 저녁식사의 마무리로는 더할 나위 없이 그만이었다.

비빈가 798번지에 위치한 킬머 식당은 화요일부터 일요일까지 매일 저녁 5시 30분에서 11시까지 저녁식사 손님을 받기 위해 문을 연다. 이곳은 매우 붐비기 때문에 반드시 예약을 해야 한다.

17. Which of the following can be said about the restaurant reviewed?

(A) It's a large restaurant in New Orleans.

(B) It serves only dinners.

(C) It is open every day of the week.

(D) It does not get crowded.

18. With what did the writer finish his meal?

(A) A cup of coffee (B) Dessert

(C) A pot of gumbo (D) Some fruit

19. What dish did the writer NOT care for?

(A) Gumbo (B) Ham

(C) Fish (D) Apple

"It's a dream to come here"
You've never seen anything quite like it-beautiful, beautiful mountains, glaciers and rivers. We're so far north, the summer is truly fascinating - 24 hours of daylight - a lot of people find it hard to believe that it does not get dark at all.
For a lot of people this is the trip of a lifetime. They come here to find the blacksmith shop their grandfather owned.
Or if it's gold you're after, I can show you everything you need to know-you can even try to pan for it.
For a golden vacation in the Canadian Yukon, call 1-403-555-1212(toll call only).

beautiful, beautiful= very beautiful / glacier 빙하
the trip of a lifetime 일생에 단 한 번 할까 말까 하는 여행 / blacksmith shop 대장간
be after 추구하다, 찾다 / pan (사금을) 채취하다, 가려내다
toll call 유료전화, 시외전화 toll call only 유료통화만 가능

"여기에 오다니 꿈만 같군요"
여러분은 이처럼 아름다운 산, 빙하와 강을 여태껏 본 적이 없을 것입니다. 우리는 북쪽으로 아주 멀리 떨어진 곳에 있습니다. 이곳 여름은 정말 환상적입니다. 24시간 내내 낮만 있습니다. 많은 사람들은 전혀 어두워지지 않는 다는 사실을 믿기 힘들겠지요.
많은 사람들에게 있어서 이곳을 찾아오는 것은 일평생 한 번 갖는 여행이 됩니다. 사람들은 여기 와서 그들의 조상들이 소유했던 대장간을 보게 됩니다.
여러분이 찾고자 하는 것이 금이라면 여러분이 알고 싶어 하는 모든 것을 보여드릴 수 있습니다. 여러분은 손수 금을 채취해 보실 수도 있습니다.
캐나다 유콘 지방에서 황금휴가를 보내실 분은 1-403-555-1212로 전화주십시오. (유료통화만 가능함).

20. What is the purpose of this article?

(A) To get people to settle in the Yukon

(B) To inform people about life in the Yukon

(C) To contact former residents of the Yukon

(D) To get people to visit the Yukon

21. What does the article promise?

(A) Wealth (B) Employment

(C) Beautiful views (D) Inexpensive living

I hope you all enjoy your lunch. We want to thank the Hilton Hotel for sponsoring our monthly luncheons. Our guest speaker this Friday will be Dr. Henry James, the author of the best-selling novel, Politics Isn't a Crime.

sponsor 후원하다 / monthly 매달의, 월례의
luncheon 오찬 monthly luncheon 월례오찬 monthly salary 월급
guest speaker 초청연사 / best-selling novel 베스트셀러 소설
crime 죄, 범죄 criminal 形 범죄의 名 범인

저는 여러분 모두가 즐거운 점심식사가 되셨길 바랍니다. 또한 우리의 월례 오찬회를 후원해 주신 힐튼호텔 측에 감사의 뜻을 전하고자 합니다. 이번 금요일의 초청연사는 베스트셀러 소설인 "정치는 범죄가 아니다"의 저자이신 헨리 제임스 박사입니다.

22. When will the speech be heard?

(A) Before lunch (B) After lunch
(C) Next month (D) Next Friday

23. How often are the luncheons held?

(A) Every Friday (B) Every month
(C) Twice a month (D) Once a year

24. What is Dr. Henry James' profession?

(A) Politician (B) Criminal
(C) Salesman (D) Author

You know how it is when you are in a faraway land. Especially when it's your first time in an unfamiliar place. That's why we go out of our way to make your stay as comfortable as possible. Our spacious rooms come complete with modern amenities and 24-hour room service. Superb restaurants, a business center, large pool and business district just minutes away add to the attraction of staying with us.

in an unfamiliar place 낯선 장소에 / That's why 그래서
go out of one's way 각별히 노력하다, 최선을 다하다
as comfortable as possible 가능한 편안하게 / spacious 넓은
come with ~에 부속되어 있다, ~을 갖추고 있다
amenities (생활을 즐겁게 해주는) 여러 설비, 쾌적한 설비
business district 상업지역 / just minutes away 불과 몇 분 거리에 있는

여러분은 멀리 떨어진 곳에 있을 때 어떤지를 알 겁니다. 특히 낯선 곳에 처음 있을 때에는 그래서 우리는 여러분이 머무시는 동안 가능한 한 편안하도록 각별히 노력합니다. 우리의 넓은 방은 현대적인 쾌적한 설비를 갖추고 있고 24시간 룸서비스를 제공합니다. 몇 분 거리 안에 있는 멋진 레스토랑, 번화가, 넓은 풀장과 상업지역은 틀림없이 우리와 함께 머물고 싶은 마음이 들게 할 것입니다.

25. What is the aim of this announcement?

(A) To make everyone feel at home

(B) To attract people' s attention

(C) To comfort men who are in an unfamiliar place

(D) To show pride in its facilities

26. How long does the room service continue?

(A) A quarter of a day (B) Twenty hours

(C) All day long (D) Several hours a day

27. Which is not include in this passage?

(A) A swimming center (B) A business center

(C) Fine restaurants (D) A department store

The Goldfish Bowl Bar is now open from 11:00 a.m. – 5:00 p.m. Lounge around the pool or sit at the bar and sip your favorite drink or try one of our special tropical "concoctions." A great place to meet great friends or business associates. For a fast and economical lunch try our special Spaghetti Bar served from 11:00 a..m. – 2:00 p.m. in the Goldfish Bowl Pasta Bar for only $4.50, Salad $1.50 an incredible value that's hard to eat.

bar 식당, 술집 / lounge 거닐다 / sip 마시다, 홀짝이다 / tropical 열대의
concoction 혼합음료 / associate 동료 / (which is) served 제공되는
an incredible value 파격적인 가격으로

골드휘시바울 식당에서는 요즘 11:00에서 5:00까지 영업합니다. 연못주위를 거닐거나 식당에 앉아 좋아하시는 술을 마시거나 우리 집 특별메뉴중의 하나인 열대산 과일들을 섞은 음료를 즐기십시오. 친구들을 만나거나 사업상의 접대를 위한 넓은 장소가 완비되었습니다. 간편하고 저렴한 점심을 드실 분은 11시 30분부터 오후 2시까지 본 식당에서 제공하는 특별 스파게티를 단돈 4.50달러에 드실 수 있고, 샐러드는 파격적인 가격인 1.50달러에 드실 수 있습니다.

28. What time is this bar open?

(A) 11:00 a..m. (B) 5:00 p.m.
(C) 11:30 a..m. (D) 5:30 p.m.

29. Where is this restaurant?

(A) Beside the pool (B) Next to the pool
(C) Around the pool (D) Over the pool

30. How much is the Spaghetti Bar?

(A) $1.50 (B) $4.50
(C) $2.00 (D) $6.00

China Palace is a restaurant for those who love Chinese food prepared and served in real Chinese style. No fancy appearances here, just good, inexpensive food. The Palace is a family-run operation and you'll meet Mr. and Mrs. Chin who greet their customers and supervise the service. The menus are printed in Chinese and English but give only the name of the dish. For more information you'll have to ask one of the Chin's and don't be surprised if you get a very detailed description!

prepared and served 조리하고 서비스하는 / in real Chinese style 정통 중국식으로
fancy appearance 겉만 번지르한 음식
a family-run operation 가족 중심으로 운영되고 있으며 / greet 접대하다

중국성은 정통 중국식으로 만들어진 중국음식을 좋아하는 사람들을 위한 식당입니다, 여기에는 겉만 번지르한 음식은 없고 값싸고 좋은 음식만이 있습니다, 이 식당은 가족중심으로 운영이 되므로 식당에서 손님을 접대하고 서비스를 감독하는 진씨 부부를 만나실 수 있습니다. 메뉴는 요리이름만 중국어와 영어로 인쇄되었습니다. 좀 더 자세한 내용은 진씨 가족 중의 한사람에게 문의하시면 상세한 설명을 듣게 될 것입니다.

31. How is food prepared at the China Palace restaurant?
    (A) In real Chinese style
    (B) In a very fancy style
    (C) The way the customer wants it
    (D) In Cantonese style

32. Who supervises the services?
    (A) The head waiter
    (B) The owner's mother, Mrs. Chin
    (C) The manager, Mr. Chin
    (D) The owner, Mr. and Mrs. Chin

33. In what language, or languages, are the menus printed?
    (A) In Chinese, of course
    (B) In English, for the tourists
    (C) In Chinese and English
    (D) In Chinese, English and Japanese

TOEIC, TOEFL, TEPS Reading Comprehension

03 항공사 승무원

Good evening, ladies and gentlemen, and welcome to Ace Airways Flight 007 to Reno, Nevada. This is your captain speaking. We are now cruising at an airspeed of 630 miles per hour and are now passing over the city of Bakersfield, California. Since we were delayed at Los Angeles International for 20 minutes, we'll be held up over Reno Airport, although it's difficult to say how long at this point. The weather report indicates that we'll be encountering a little turbulence over the Sierra ranges, and we have therefore left the seat belt light on and recommend that all passengers keep their seat belts fastened. Please remember that federal regulations now prohibit smoking on all domestic flights, and this includes inside the lavatories. We invite you to take advantage of the free-drink service we are offering passengers on this flight. Relax and enjoy your flight.

This is your captain speaking 저는 기장입니다
at an airspeed of 630 miles per hour 시속 630마일 속도로
hold up 연착하다, 늦추다
The weather report indicates that 일기예보에 의하면(따르면), indicates = says
turbulence (대기의) 난류 / the Sierra ranges 시에라 산맥
leave the seat belt light on 안전벨트 불이 켜져 있다. / prohibit ~ing ~을 금하다
Relax and enjoy your flight. 편안하고 즐거운 여행이 되십시오.

신사, 숙녀 여러분 안녕하십니까. 네바다주 르노행 에이스항공 007편을 이용해 주신 여러분을 환영합니다. 저는 여러분이 타신 비행기의 기장입니다. 우리는 지금 캘리포니아, 베이커스필드시 상공을 시속 630마일 속도로 비행하고 있습니다. 로스앤젤레스 국제 공항에서 20분간 지연됐기 때문에 르노공항에 연착할 것 같습니다. 그러나 지금 상황에선 얼마나 연착이 될 것이라고 말씀드리기는 어렵습니다. 일기예보에 따르면 시에라 산맥

상공에서 약간의 대기난류를 만날 수 있다고 하므로 안전벨트 불이 켜져 있으니 모든 승객들은 안전벨트를 착용하시길 바랍니다. 연방규정에 따라 모든 국내선에서 흡연은 금지한다는 사실을 유념해 주십시오. 또한 이 규정은 화장실 안에서도 적용됩니다. 저희 항공기에서 승객여러분께 제공하는 무료 음료수 서비스를 마음껏 이용하시길 바랍니다. 편안하고 즐거운 비행이 되십시오.

34. Where are they going?

(A) Bakersfield (B) Los Angeles

(C) Reno (D) California

35. Why will they be arriving late?

(A) They will encounter turbulence.

(B) They were held up in Los Angeles.

(C) There are new federal regulations.

(D) It is difficult to say at this point.

36. What did the speaker recommend?

(A) Confining smoking to smoking section

(B) Releasing seat belts

(C) Having a drink

(D) Ordering a free meal

Here's something you've been waiting for an opportunity to vacation in the sun at a price that's truly within your budget. Blue Pacific Air, the no-nonsense airline, offers you a first class five-day vacation package at a price so low that it's less than the normal airfare alone. We'll take you to Guam in comfort, accommodate you in style, and relaxed. Call now for information that will bring summer's warmth to your winter chills.

at a price that's truly within your budget 정말로 당신 예산 범위 안의 비용으로
no-nonsense 덤핑이 아닌, 신용 있는 / vacation package 휴가 상품
in comfort 편안하게 / accommodate 숙박시키다 / in style 품위 있게
will bring summer's warmth to your winter chills 겨울 추위에 여름의 따뜻함을 전해 드릴

순수하게 당신의 예산범위 안의 비용으로 태양아래에서 여름휴가를 보낼 수 있는 기회를 기다려 왔다면 바로 여기에 있습니다. 덤핑이 아닌 신용 있는 항공사 불루 퍼시픽 항공은 보통 항공료보다 더 저렴한 가격으로 5일 일정 최고급 휴가를 여러분께 제공합니다. 여러분을 편안하게 괌까지 모셔 품위 있는 숙박시설을 제공하여 편안하게 해 드릴 것입니다. 지금 문의하시면 당신의 겨울 추위에 여름의 따뜻함을 전해드릴 정보를 드리겠습니다.

37. What is the name of the airline?

(A) Pacific Airways　　(B) Royal Pacific Air
(C) Blue Water Airways　　(D) Blue Pacific Air

38. What are they advertising?

(A) A no-nonsense trip　　(B) A five-day vacation
(C) The normal airfare　　(D) A trip to Hawaii

Attention, please. Attention, please. All personnel will report to the south lawn for morning exercise. Supervisors will accompany their work teams. The exercise session will begin at 10:30 and end at 11:00.

attention, please 알려 드립니다. / personnel 직원, 요원 / report 출두하다, 집합하다
supervisor 감독관, 담당자 / accompany ~에 배치되다, ~에 동반되다

알려드립니다. 모든 직원은 아침운동을 하러 남쪽잔디밭으로 나오십시오. 각 팀별로 담당자가 배치될 것입니다. 운동은 10시 30분에 시작하여 11시에 끝날 것입니다.

39. Who will participate in the exercises?

(A) All personnel (B) Only the workers
(C) Only the supervisors (D) Only the management

40. How long will the session last?

(A) Thirty minutes (B) One hour
(C) One hour and a half (D) All morning

41. Where will the exercises take place?

(A) In the south gym (B) On the lawn
(C) In the parking lot (D) In the lobby

Gopher Golf Club, exclusively for members representing various professions, now has opening for new members due to the relocation of five of its members to another State. New members will be accepted on a first-come basis, subject to the approval of the Club board members. So, join us now in order to enjoy a few good games before winter sets in.

exclusively 엄선된, 전문적인 / profession 전문직
on a first-come basis 선착순으로 / subject to (~을 얻는 것을) 조건으로 하여
board member (단체의) 이사 / set in (일, 계절 등이) 시작되다

이번에 다양한 전문직을 대표하는 회원들로 엄선된 고퍼 골프클럽에서는 기존의 회원 중 다섯 분이 다른 주로 이사 가셨기 때문에 새로운 회원을 맞이하고자 합니다. 새로운 회원은 클럽 이사들의 동의를 거쳐 선착순으로 입회하실 것입니다. 그러니 겨울이 시작되기 전에 저희와 함께 좋은 경기를 즐기실 분은 지금 신청하십시오.

42. Who is eligible to join the Gopher Golf Club?

(A) Five new people

(B) Representative of the professions

(C) Professional golfers

(D) Those approved by the board

43. How are new members selected?

(A) On a first-come basis

(B) According to profession

(C) Open competition

(D) Subject to approval of the Club board

Why not rent-a-car? Top quality cars at the lowest prices are offered by Voll Rent-a-car. Sedans automatic and manuals range in price from $23 per day including unlimited kilometers, free delivery and pick-up, plus insurance. All cars are covered by 24 hour road service by the NRSC (National Road Service Company). This company has offices throughout America, so locating Voll Rent-a-car easily interstate. Miami 19a Darlinghurst Road, King Gate. Phone 321-5744 and our western branch 322-7452.

automatic 자동의 / manual 수동의 / range ~의 범위에 걸치다
unlimited kilometers 거리 무제한 / free delivery and pick-up 무료 인도, 인수
insurance 보험료 / road service 노상정비 서비스 / office=branch 지점, 사무실
locate ~의 위치를 찾아내다, / interstate 주 사이에서

자동차를 빌리지 않으시렵니까? 볼 렌터카에서 고급 차를 저렴한 가격으로 빌려드립니다. 하루에 23달러에서부터 다양한 수동 변속형 및 자동 변속형 세단이 준비되어 있고 거리에 제한을 두지 않으며, 무료로 갖다드리고 찾아오고 보험료가 포함되어 있습니다. 모든 차는 전국노상서비스회사 NRSC(National Road Service Company)의 24시간 순회서비스를 받을 수 있습니다. 이 회사는 미국 전역에 걸쳐 지점이 있기 때문에 자동차로 여행하시고자 하시는 분은 손쉽게 각 주에 있는 볼 렌터카를 이용하실 수 있습니다.
주소 : 킹스게이트, 다아링허스트가, 마이애미19a, 전화 : 321-5744 서북지점
전화 : 322-7452

44. Which of the following is not included in the service by Voll Rent-a-car?

(A) Free delivery and pick-up

(B) Unlimited kilometers

(C) Insurance

(D) Free repair system

45. What kind of service is presented by NRSC?

(A) Renting all kinds of cars

(B) Helping the renters find the near repair shop

(C) Free delivery and pick-up

(D) Driving for the rentees

46. What is the telephone number of Voll Ren-a-car western branch?

(A) 321-5744 (B) 322-7452

(C) 312-7545 (D) 312-4572

This week, Travelers' Inn offers its guests a "power-start" breakfast in addition to our usual complimentary morning service between the hours of 6:00 and 8:30 a.m. The breakfast includes juice, scrambled eggs and toast with butter and jam. As usual, the complimentary morning service includes coffee or tea, a copy of the morning paper. To receive this free service, simply inform the front desk before 11:30 the preceding night. Once again, thank you for choosing Traveler's Inn as your place to stay.

in addition to ~에 더하여 / complimentary 우대의, 무료의
a copy of the morning paper 조간신문 한 부.

이번 주에 여행자호텔에서는 손님들에게 오전 6시에서 8시 30분 사이에 서비스되는 일상적인 무료아침 식사 외에 "파우어스타트"라는 아침식사가 제공됩니다. 아침식사에는 주스, 풀어 끓인 달걀 그리고 버터와 잼을 바른 토스트가 포함됩니다. 평상시에 일상적인 아침 서비스에는 커피 또는 홍차 그리고 조간 신문 1부가 포함됩니다. 이 서비스는 무료로 받을 수 있습니다. 단지 그전날 밤 11시 30분 전에 프런트에 알려 주시기만 하면 됩니다. 다시 한 번 숙박지로서 여행자 호텔을 선택하신 것을 감사드립니다.

47. What is special offer this week?

(A) A free newspaper (B) Morning service

(C) A meal (D) Complimentary coffee or tea

48. How can a guest receive this service?

(A) Fill in the application form.

(B) Go to the dining hall between 6:00 and 8:30 a. m..

(C) Turn in the complimentary service coupon.

(D) Tell the desk the night before.

Attention, please. We'd like to notify all passengers on Flight Pan Am 666 to Amsterdam and Paris that due to a delay with a connecting flight from San Francisco, Flight 666 will leave at 13:50 instead of 11:50. We'd also like to notify passengers boarding that flight that will leave from gate No. 10, instead of gate No. 16. We apologize for any inconvenience.

passengers boarding 탑승객
for any inconvenience 여러 가지 불편을 끼쳐드려서.

암스테르담과 파리로 가는 팬암 666편에 탑승하실 승객 여러분에게 알려드립니다. 샌프란시스코 공항에서 출발하는 환승편이 지연되므로 666편은 11시 50분이 아닌 1시 50분에 출발하겠습니다. 또한 비행기는 16번 출구가 아니라 10번 출구에서 떠나게 됨을 탑승객들에게 알려드립니다. 여러 가지 불편을 끼쳐서 죄송합니다.

49. Flight 666 is delayed by how long?

(A) It's delayed by one hour.

(B) It's very delayed.

(C) It's delayed by two hours.

(D) It's over delayed.

50. Which gate was it supposed to have left from?

(A) Gate 6 (B) Gate 11

(C) Gate 16 (D) Gate 10

51. Who is the most likely person to be making this announcement?

(A) A pilot (B) A purser

(C) A technician (D) An announcer

Good afternoon, ladies and gentlemen. Welcome aboard flight 325 to Bangkok. We'll be flying at an altitude 23,000 feet, and should arrive in Bangkok at 6:45. We hope you have an enjoyable trip.

Welcome aboard 탑승해 주셔서 감사합니다
at an altitude 23,000 feet 고도 23,000피트로.

신사 숙녀 여러분 안녕하십니까. 방콕 행 325편을 탑승해 주셔서 감사합니다. 우리는 23,000피트의 고도로 날아서 6시 45분에 방콕에 도착하겠습니다. 즐거운 여행이 되시기를 바랍니다.

52. Where is the speaker?

(A) On a ship (B) On a train
(C) On a plane (D) On a bus

53. When will they get to Bangkok?

(A) 2:30 (B) 3:25
(C) 5:20 (D) 6:45

Good afternoon ladies and gentleman. This is the captain speaking. We expect to be encountering some heavy turbulence shortly. Please return to your seats and fasten your safety belts until further announcements. We apologize for any inconvenience.

This is the captain speaking. 저는 기장입니다 / heavy turbulence 심한 난기류. fasten your safety belts 안전벨트를 매다.

신사 숙녀 여러분 안녕하십니까. 저는 기장입니다, 우리는 곧 강한 난기류를 만날 것이라 예상됩니다, 좌석으로 돌아가셔서 다음 안내방송이 있을 때까지 안전벨트를 매고 계시길 부탁드립니다. 불편을 끼쳐드려 죄송합니다.

54. Where is this?

(A) On a train (B) On a ship

(C) On an airplane (D) On this subway

55. When can everyone unfasten their seat belts?

(A) When the turbulence is over.

(B) When they are told that they may.

(C) Shortly

(D) When the turbulence begins.

Ladies and Gentlemen, we have arrived at New York, John F. Kennedy International Airport, where the local time is now five minutes to noon. For your safety, please remain seated until the aircraft comes to a complete stop. Please be sure to take all of your belongings when you disembark. We would like to thank you for flying with us today. We look forward to having the pleasure of serving you again, and wish you a pleasant stay here in New York. Thank you.

the local time 현지시간 / belongings 소지품 / disembark (비행기, 배 등에서) 내리다.

신사 숙녀 여러분, 뉴욕 존 F.케네디 국제공항에 도착했습니다. 현지시간은 11시 55분입니다. 여러분의 안전을 위해 항공기가 완전히 멈출 때까지 자리에 앉아 계시길 바랍니다. 내리실 때에는 모든 소지품을 꼭 챙겨 주십시오, 오늘도 저희 비행기를 이용해 주셔서 감사드립니다. 다시 여러분을 모시길 바라며, 여기 뉴욕에서 즐겁게 머무르시길 바랍니다. 감사합니다.

56. What time does the plane arrive?

(A) 12:15　　(B) 11:55

(C) 12:00　　(D) 12:15\

57. Who could make this announcement?

(A) A guide　　(B) A stewardess

(C) A crewman　　(D) A passenger

The bus for Cleveland is now arriving in lane number 8. Passengers for Chicago should take their baggage to gate 10 and begin boarding. Have your tickets ready. This is the last call for the bus to Detroit from Lane 13. All passengers should be aboard. The bus from New York is going to be about 30 minutes late. When it arrives we will announce the lane number.

클리브랜드행 버스가 이제 8번 선에 도착하겠습니다. 시카고행 승객 여러분은 수하물 10번 출구로 운반하고 승차해 주시길 바랍니다. 승차권은 미리 준비하여 주십시오, 13번 선에서 떠날 디트로이트행 버스에 대한 마지막 방송입니다. 모든 승객은 탑승해 주십시오, 뉴욕에서 오는 버스는 30분 정도 늦어질 예정입니다. 이 버스가 도착했을 때 노선 번호를 안내해 드리겠습니다.

58. If you are going to Detroit, where should you be now?

(A) Waiting at gate 10 (B) Waiting in the lounge

(C) Standing at lane 13 (D) On the bus

59. If you are waiting for a friend from New York, ________________.

(A) you will have to wait a little at lounge

(B) you should go to lane 30

(C) you should go to gate 13

(D) you should go to the baggage gate

Good afternoon ladies and gentlemen. This is your Greyhound coach service to Dallas, Texas. I am your driver, Bill Johnson, and I'll be with you all the way to El Paso. This bus is airconditioned for your comfort. Please do not open the windows. If you feel too hot or too cold, please tell me and I'll try and adjust the temperature for you. There is a rest-room at the rear. Our next stop there for approximately 45 minutes. We'll be there in about 4 hours from now, that is about 10:30 A.M. Thank you for your attention.

신사 숙녀 여러분 안녕하십니까. 이것은 택사스주의 달라스로 가는 그레이하운드 고속버스입니다. 저는 엘파소까지 모든 길을 여러분과 함께 할 운전사 빌입니다. 이 버스는 여러분의 쾌적함을 위해 냉난방장치가 완비되어 있습니다. 그러니 창문을 열지 마십시오. 만약 너무 덥거나 춥다고 느끼실 때에는 저에게 말씀하십시오.

60. Where is the speaker?

(A) On a ship (B) On a bus
(C) On a train (D) On a taxi

61. What is the final destination?

(A) Oklahoma City (B) California
(C) Dallas (D) El Paso

63. What should a passenger do if he feels too hot?

(A) Open the window. (B) Stop the driver.
(C) Speak to the driver. (D) Adjust the temperature.

Paging Mr. Brown, Mr. Brown of room number 1451, please. We have an urgent overseas telephone call for Mr. Brown. Mr. Brown to the Reception Desk, please.

64. Where would this announcement be heard?

(A) In a airport (B) In a restaurant

(C) In a hotel lobby (D) Over an aircraft intercom

65. What should Mr. Brown do?

(A) Go to the front desk immediately.

(B) Answer the nearest telephone.

(C) Go to room 1451.

(D) Call overseas.

DEPARTURES			
FLIGHT NUMBER	GATE	TIME	DEPARTING FOR
228	15	13:15	Beirut / Bombay
183	18	13:40	Mexico City
667	14	14:00	London/Frankfurt
24	16	15:35	Rabat
819	15	16:10	Bombay
444	14	17:20	Delhi / Bombay

66. The direct flight to Bombay this afternoon is number ________.

(A) 24 (B) 228

(C) 444 (D) 819

67. The passengers going to Rabat should go to Gate ________.

(A) 14 (B) 15

(C) 16 (D) 18

Hotel	Standard Rate	Weekend Rate	Benefits
Drake	$205	$145	Cocktails, refreshments, continental breakfast
Hilton	$245	$125	Double room in the towers, dinner
Mayfair Regent	$195	$125	Parking
Nikko	$215	$99	Parking
Palmer House	$135	$75	Continental breakfast
Ritz-Carlton	$250	$215	Full breakfast, parking
Swiss Grand	$350	$199	Executive suite, late checkout, parking

68. Of these hotels, which is the most expensive?

(A) Ritz-Carlton (B) Hilton

(C) Drake (D) Nikko

69. Which is the least expensive hotel?

(A) Swiss Grand (B) Ritz-Carlton

(C) Palmer House (D) Nikko

70. Which is the least expensive hotel?

(A) Palmer House (B) Nikko

(C) Mayfair Regent (D) Drake

호텔	정상요금	주말요금	특전
드레이크	205불	145불	칵테일, 다과, 가벼운 아침식사
힐튼	245불	125불	고층의 2인실, 정찬
네이페어 리젠트	195불	125불	주차
니코	215불	99불	주차
파머 하우스	135불	75불	가벼운 아침식사
리츠-칼튼	250불	215불	아침 정식, 주차
스위스 그랜드	350불	199불	응접실, 늦은 퇴실, 주차

Intercity Europe	Rail time	Air time
Paris to Amsterdam	5 hr	1 hr
Paris to Madrid	13 hr	1 hr, 50 min
Paris to Nice	7 hr	1 hr, 20 min
Frankfurt to Rome	12 hr	1 hr, 45 min
Frankfurt to Brussels	5 hr, 30 min	1 hr
Frankfurt to Vienna	9 hr	1 hr, 20 min
London to Edinburgh	4 hr, 30 min	1 hr, 15 min
London to Paris	5 hr, 30 min	1 hr, 5 min

71. Which city is closest to Paris by air?

(A) London (B) Nice

(C) Amsterdam (D) Madrid

72. Which two cities are the furthest apart by rail?

(A) Paris to Madrid

(B) Paris and Nice

(C) Frankfurt and Rome

(D) Frankfurt and Vienna

73. How long does it take from Frankfurt to Brussels?

(A) 1 hour by rail (B) 1 hour by air

(C) 5 hours by rail (D) 5 hours by air

74. What is the longest flight?

(A) Paris to Madrid (B) Frankfurt to Rome

(C) Paris to Nice (D) London to Edinburgh

75. 빈칸에 들어갈 가장 알맞은 것을 고르시오.

Changes in heating systems of buildings can also lead to disease. In the 1970s, there was a worldwide shortage of heating oil. To save fuel, hotels in the United States lowered the temperature in their heating systems. This lower temperature was just perfect for a deadly germ which grows in heating pipes. When the heated air was blown into the rooms of a hotel, it carried ______. Many visitors became ill and several died.

shortage 부족 / deadly 치명적인 / germ 병원균
perfect 완전한, 더할 나위 없는, 최적의 / heated 뜨거워진.

건물의 난방 시설이 바뀌면 병을 유발할 수도 있다. 1970년대에 전 세계적으로 난방유가 부족할 때가 있었다. 연료를 절약하기 위해서 미국 내 호텔들은 난방시설의 온도를 낮추었다. 이 낮아진 온도는 난방 파이프에 서식하는 치명적인 병원균에게 최적의 온도였다. 뜨거워진 공기가 호텔 방안으로 들어가, 병원균을 옮겼다. 많은 방문객들이 병에 걸렸고, 몇 명은 사망도 했다.

(A) heating oil (B) lower temperature

(C) the germs (D) heating pipes

■ 다음 글을 읽고 물음에 답하시오. (TOEIC)

SPICED LEMON TEA

3 cups	boiling water	6	tea bags
3 sticks	cinnamon	1/4 teaspoon	ground cloves
1/8 teaspoon	ground nutmeg	2/3 cup	sugar
11/2 cups	cold water		
Juice of 3 lemons (about 1/2 cup)		Ice cubes	

Pour boiling water over tea bags, cinnamon, cloves and nutmeg ; Steep 5 minutes. Remove tea bags and cinnamon sticks. Stir in sugar, cold water and lemon juice ; Chill. Serve over ice with cinnamon stick, if desired.
Makes about 5 1/3 cups.

cinnamon 계피 / clove 정향(꽃봉오리를 말린 향료) / nutmeg 육두구(열대산 상록수)
steep (액체에) 담그다, 적시다 / chill 식히다.

향료를 곁들인 레몬차

끓는 물 3컵.	찻봉지 6개
계피 3쪽	1/4 찻숟가락 정향가루
1/8 찻숟가락 육두구가루	2/3 컵 설탕
1과 1/2컵 찬물	
3가지 레몬주스(약1/2컵)	얼음

찻봉지, 계피 정향, 육두구에 끓는 물을 붓고 5분 간 담근다. 찻봉지와 계피를 제거한다. 설탕과 찬물, 레몬주스를 넣어 젓는다. 식힌다. 만약 찬 것을 원하면 얼음과 계피를 더한다. 5와 1/3컵이 된다.

76. How many procedures are required to make a cup of lemon tea?

(A) 2 (B) 3

(C) 4 (D) 5

77. Which of the ingredients is added last?

(A) nutmeg (B) hot water

(C) tea bags (D) lemon juice

78. How many cups of lemon tea can you make with 3 times the amount of these ingredients?

(A) 12 (B) 14

(C) 16 (D) 18

79. 빈칸에 들어갈 가장 알맞은 것을 고르시오(9급 행정).

Eating candy can produce acids in the body. Consuming carbohydrates can even produce an alcoholic condition in your body. One of our great orators, William Jennings Bryan, gave speeches nationwide about the bad effects of drinking alcohol, causing more than one person to change his drinking habits. ______, Bryan himself died of an alcoholic stomach as a result of eating thirteen pancakes with syrup for breakfast. Eating the pancakes, which are full of carbohydrates, and the sugary syrup, created a kind of alcoholic brew in his stomach. This innocently consumed brew produced alcoholic poisoning, which in turn led to his death.

(A) Consequently (B) Ironically

(C) Besides (D) Accordingly

acid 산 / carbohydrate 탄수화물 / nationwide 전국적으로
brew 양조주(음료) / innocently 단순히

사탕을 먹으면 체내에 산이 생성될 수 있다. 탄수화물을 소비하면 심지어 당신의 몸속에 알코올이 만들어질 수도 있다. 한 유명한 연설가인 윌리엄 제닝스 브라이언은 술을 마셔서 생기는 나쁜 영향들에 대해 전국적으로 연설을 했는데, 이로 인해 한 명 이상의 사람이 음주 습관을 바꾸게 되었다. 얄궂게도 브라이언은 시럽을 친 13개의 팬케이크를 아침으로 먹고 알코올로 인한 위통으로 죽었다. 탄수화물로 가득 찬 팬케이크와 설탕 시럽을 먹자 위에 일종의 알코올이 생성된 것이었다. 모르는 사이에 소비된 알코올은 중독을 일으켰고, 이는 또한 그를 죽게 했다.

80. 다음 글을 읽고 본문 전체의 흐름과 관계가 없는 문장을 고르시오.

A healthy diet is important for children as well as adults. ① When adults have poor eating habits, their children usually do, too. ② After all, children eat the same way as their parents do. ③ We know that the food we eat affects us in different ways. ④ When parents eat healthy food, the children will think it tastes good.

eating habits 식습관 / healthy food 건강식품

건강 식품은 성인들뿐만 아니라 어린이들에게도 중요하다. ① 어른들이 잘못된 식습관을 갖고 있으면, 그들의 아이들 또한 보통 그렇다. ② 결국 아이들은 자신들의 부모와 같은 방식으로 먹는다. ③ 우리가 먹는 음식물이 여러 가지 방법으로 우리에게 영향을 끼친다는 것을 우리는 안다. ④ 부모들이 건강식품을 먹을 때 아이들은 그것이 맛있을 것이라고 생각할 것이다.

■ 다음 광고를 읽고 물음에 답하시오. (TOEIC)

A Review : Kilmer's Kitchen
Kilmer's Kitchen isn't very large, but the food is good. Kilmer Ragley does the cooking and his menu includes a lot of New Orleans French favorites. When I was there I had gumbo. This tasty mixture of ham and fish is cooked in a heavy pot. I thought it was delicious. For dessert I had apple surprise, a mixture of cooked apples and dough. It was too sweet for me, but you might like it if you have a taste for sweets. Kilmer has different kinds of coffee, and my espresso was a perfect end to a good dinner.
Kilmer's Kitchen, at 798 Bourbon Street, opens for dinner every evening from 5:30 to 11:00, Tuesday through Sunday. The restaurant gets very busy, so be sure to make a reservation before you go.

do the cooking 요리하다, 주방장이다 / favorites=favorite foods 특별요리, 특미
gumbo 오크라를 넣은 진한 수프 / tasty mixture 맛있는 혼합요리 / pot 냄비
dough 가루 반죽 / have a taste for ~을 좋아하다
espresso 커피의 일종(가루를 스팀에 쐬어 진하게 만듬)
perfect end to a good dinner 맛있는 저녁을 완벽하게 끝내는 후식
be sure to 틀림없이, 확실히.

81. Which of the following can be said about the restaurant reviewed?

(A) It's a large restaurant in New Orleans.

(B) It serves only dinners.

(C) It is open every day of the week.

(D) It does not get crowded.

82. With what did the writer finish his meal?

(A) A cup of coffee (B) Dessert

(C) A pot of gumbo (D) Some fruit

83. What dish did the writer NOT care for?

(A) Gumbo (B) Ham

(C) Fish (D) Apple

MENU

(All prices : add 10% sales tax)

Pizza		Topping	
Large Pizza	$ 13.00	Vegetables	$ .75
Medium Pizza	$ 10.00	Mushrooms	$ .75
Small Pizza	$ 7.00	Pepperoni	$ .75
One Piece	$ 2.00		
Salad		**Beverage & Drinks**	
Italian	$ 2.50	Orange Juice	$ 1.50
French	$ 2.50	Large Coke	$ 1.00
Greek	$ 2.50	Medium Coke	$ .75
		Small Coke	$ .50
		Sprite	$ .75

84. If a customer orders a Large Pizza with a topping of mushrooms and vegetables, Italian Salad and a Large Coke, how much would she/he pay including sales tax? (TEPS)

(a) $16.50 (b) $18.00

(c) $18.70 (d) $19.80

메뉴(모든 메뉴의 정가에 10%의 세금이 부과됨)

피자	$13.00	토핑	
피자(大)	$10.00	야채	$.75
피자(中)	$7.00	버섯	$.75
피자(小)	$2.00	페페로니	$.75
한 조각			
샐러드		음료수	
이탈리안	$2.50	오렌지 주스	$1.50
프렌치	$2.50	콜라(大)	$1.00
그리스	$2.50	콜라(中)	$.75
		콜라(小)	$.50
		스프라이트	$.75

■ Answer the following questions. (동덕여대)
Question 10–13 refer the following recipe.

Omelette Supreme : 6 eggs, an onion, a green bell pepper, some mushrooms, 2 slices of Swiss cheese, some milk, salt, black pepper and butter.
Kitchen implements : a standard frying pan, a bowl, a knife and a spatula
Crack the eggs and put their contents in the bowl. Add a cup of milk and a pinch of salt and pepper. Blend the eggs and milk into a uniform yellow color.
Coat the bottom of the frying pan with some butter. Once the butter has melted pour in the egg batter. After spreading it out evenly, turn the gas on low and let cook for about 5 minutes.
While the mixture cooks, chop the vegetables. Then lay one slice of cheese on top of the cooking egg. Next put all the pieces of vegetables on top of the cheese and egg. Then place the second slice of cheese over the vegetables.

Use a spatula to carefully flip half of circle of egg batter over so it covers the vegetables and congeals with the bottom lip if egg. Let cook for 10 more minutes. After five minutes turn over the entire omelette and let the other side cook until it turns a golden shade. then enjoy.

spatula 주걱 / contents 내용물 / pinch 조금, 한 번 집은 양
until it turns a golden shade 노릇해질 때까지.

최고의 오믈렛 요리
요리재료 : 달걀 6개, 양파1개, 피망1개, 버섯 약간, 치즈 2조각, 우유 약간, 소금, 후추, 버터
주방도구 : 표준형 프라이팬, 주발, 칼, 주걱
달걀을 깨서 내용물을 주발에 넣는다. 우유 한 컵과 소량의 소금과 후추를 첨가한다. 잘 젓는다. 달걀과 우유를 섞어 저어서 일정한 노란 색깔이 나도록 한다. 프라이팬에 약간 버터를 바른다. 녹인 버터를 달걀 반죽에 뿌린다. 반죽을 고르게 펴고 나서 낮은 불로 가스레인지를 켜고 약 5분 동안 익힌다. 익히는 동안 야채를 썬다. 그러고 나서 조리하고 있는 달걀 위에 있는 치즈 한 조각을 얹는다. 다음에 치즈와 달걀 위에 야채 조각들을 모두 뿌린다. 그러고 나서 그 야채 조각들을 모두 뿌린다. 그러고 나서 그 야채 위에 두 번째 치즈 조각을 얹는다. 주걱을 사용해서 조심스럽게 원형의 달걀 반죽을 반으로 뒤집어 포개지게 한다. 그렇게 해서 야채를 덮도록 하고 밑바닥 부분의 달걀 가장자리 부분과 함께 응고시킨다. 그러고 나서 10분 더 익힌다. 5분이 지나면 오믈렛을 통째로 뒤집어서 반대쪽이 노릇노릇해질 때까지 익히고 나서 맛있게 먹으면 된다.

85. What is added to the eggs in the bowl before stirring?

(A) Milk (B) Butter
(C) A bell pepper (D) One slices cheese

86. How should the vegetables be prepared before being added to the pan?

(A) They should be boiled.
(B) They should be cut up.

(C) They should be marinated.

(D) They should be seasoned with salt and pepper in a bowl.

87. How much time should pass before adding cheese?

(A) 5 minutes (B) 10 minutes

(C) 15 minutes (D) 20 minutes

88. When should the mushrooms be added?

① After the onions

② Before the bell pepper

③ before the second slice of cheese

④ At the same time as the salt and pepper

■ (14~16) 다음 글을 읽고 물음에 답하시오.(홍익대)

During the summer you should be even more careful than usual of the foods you prepare. Foods spoil faster in hot weather than in cold weather. When you are shopping, purchase frozen and refrigerated foods last. Don't make long stops on the way home, because things may become soft or warm. Using insulated bags helps keep food cold until you can get home; milk and milk products should be refrigerated immediately. When camping or picnicking, or at any time when refrigeration isn't available use special dry foods. Don't leave foods in a hot car or a beach bag. Picnic favorites like meat, chicken and egg salad should be kept in a cooler. Above all if food doesn't seem to be normal in appearance, discard it immediately. Don't taste it.

frozen and refrigerated foods 냉동, 냉장 식품 / milk products 유제품
refrigerate 냉장(냉동)하다 / insulated 절연된, 격리된 / cooler 냉장고
discard 버리다 / in appearance 보기에는, 외관은.

여름에는 여러분이 준비한 음식들에 대해 평소보다 훨씬 더 조심해야 한다. 음식물은 추운 날씨보다 더운 날씨에서 더 빨리 상한다. 쇼핑할 때는 냉동냉장 음식들을 마지막에 구입하도록 하라. 음식물이 물러지거나 열을 받을 수도 있기 때문에 집으로 오는 동안에 오랫동안 머물렀다 가지 말라. 열 차단 쇼핑백을 사용하면 집에 갈 때까지 음식을 신선하게 유지하는데 도움이 된다. 그리고 우유와 유제품은 즉시 냉장고에 보관해야만 한다. 캠핑이나 소풍을 갈 때나 냉장고를 이용할 수 없을 때는 특별히 건조된 음식들을 사용하라. 더운 차 안이나 비치백 속에 음식을 남겨두지 말라. 고기, 닭고기 · 달걀 샐러드 같은 피크닉 선호 음식들은 냉장고 안에 보관해야 한다. 무엇보다도, 음식이 보기에 정상적인 것 같지 않으면 즉시 버려라. 그것을 먹지 마라.

89. What is the main topic of the passage?

(A) How to keep food from spoiling during the summer

(A) How to prepare food in hot weather

(A) The problem of food poisoning

(A) The problem of indigestion in summer

90. Which of the following would be least likely to spoil in warm weather?

(A) Fresh vegetables and fruits

(B) Dry soup mix

(C) Milk and dairy products

(D) Meat and chicken

91. According to the talk what should you do with food that doesn't seem to be normal?

(A) Put it in the refrigerator (B) Consume immediately

(C) Throw it away instantly (D) Taste it

1. C	2. D	3. B	4. B	5. C	6. A	7. C	8. B	9. C	10. C
11. D	12. B	13. A	14. C	15. B	16. D	17. B	18. A	19. D	20. D
21. C	22. B	23. B	24. D	25. B	26. C	27. D	28. A	29. C	30. B
31. A	32. D	33. C	34. C	35. B	36. C	37. D	38. B	39. A	40. A
41. B	42. B	43. D	44. D	45. B	46. B	47. C	48. D	49. C	50. D
51. D	52. C	53. D	54. C	55. B	56. B	57. B	58. D	59. A	60. B
61. C	62.A	63. C	64. C	65. A	66. D	67. C	68. A	69. B	70. A
71. C	72. A	73. B	74. A	75. C	76. D	77. D	78. C	79. B	80. C
81. B	82. A	83. D	84. D	85. B	86. B	87. D	88. D	89. A	90. B
91. C									

English Sayings and Proverbs

English Sayings and Proverbs
영어 격언 및 속담

영어로 속담을 알아두면 매우 유용하게 사용할 수 있다. 속담은 매우 복잡한 뜻도 단 몇 마디로 표현할 수 있도록 해줄 뿐만 아니라 무엇보다도 그 나라의 속담을 사용하면 상대방과 더욱 친근해질 수 있기 때문이다. 이것이 한 나라의 원수가 다른 나라를 방문하여 연설할 때 자주 그 나라의 속담을 인용하는 이유일 것이다. 또한 자격증 면접시험 및 필기시험에서도 가끔 출제가 되고 있으니 기억하고 있으면 많은 도움이 될 것이다.

1. A buddy from my old stomping grounds. 죽마고우
2. Adding insult to injury. 엎친 데 덮친다.
3. A drop in the bucket. 코끼리 비스킷
4. A friend in need is a friend indeed.
   어려울 때 친구가 진짜 친구다.
5. After the storm comes the calm.
   비온 뒤에 땅이 굳어진다.
6. A good medicine tastes bitter.
   입에 쓴 약이 병에는 좋다.
7. A journey of a thousand miles begins with a single step.
   천릿길도 한 걸음부터
8. A little knowledge is dangerous. 선 무당이 사람 잡는다.
9. A loaf of bread is better than the song of many birds.
   금강산도 식후경
10. A man is known by the company he keeps.
    사람은 그가 사귀는 친구를 보면 알 수 있다.
11. A man of many talents. 팔방미인
12. Among the blind, the one-eyed is King.
    장님 사이에서는 애꾸가 왕이다.

13. As one sows, so shall he reap.
콩 심은 데 콩 나고 팥 심은 데 팥 난다.

14. A rags to riches story. 개천에서 용 났다.

15. A rat in a trap. 독 안에 든 쥐

16. A rolling stone gathers no moss.
구르는 돌에는 이끼가 끼지 않는다.

17. A soft answer turned away wrath. 웃는 낯에 침 뱉으랴.

18. As poor as a church mouse. 찢어지게 가난하다.

19. As the twig is bent, so grows the tree.
될성부른 나무는 떡잎부터 알아본다.

20. A stitch in time saves nine.
호미로 막을 데 가래로 막는다.

21. Be it ever so humble, there's no place like home.
아무리 비천할지라도 집만 한 곳은 없다.

22. Better be the head of a dog than the tail of a lion.
소의 꼬리가 되느니보다는 닭의 머리가 되는 게 낫다.

23. Beauty is in the eye of the beholder.
제 눈에 안경이다.

24. Bad news travels quickly.
나쁜 소식은 빨리 퍼진다.

25. Between a rock and a hard place. 진퇴양난

26. Birds of a feather flock together.
가재는 게 편이라./유유상종

27. Blood is thicker than water.
피는 물보다 진하다.

28. Born in a barn. 꼬리가 길다.

29. Can't get blood from a turnip.
벼룩의 간을 빼먹는다.

30. Casting pearls before swine. 돼지에게 진주

31. Castle in the air. 공중누각

32. Charity begins at home. 팔이 안으로 굽는다.

33. Clothes make the man. 옷이 날개라.

34. Cut off your nose to spite your face.
누워서 침 뱉기

35. Do good and don't look back.
선을 행하고 뒤를 돌아보지 마라.

36. Do into others as you would have them into you.
자신이 대접받길 원하는 것처럼 타인을 대접하라.

37. Don't back him into a corner.
개도 나갈 구멍을 보고 쫓아라.

38. Don't count your chickens before they hatch.
김칫국부터 마신다.

39. Don't mount a dead horse.
이미 결정된 일로 왈가왈부하지 마라.

40. Early to bed and early to rise makes a man healthy, and wise.
일찍 자고 일찍 일어나면 사람이 건강해지고 현명해 진다.

41. Even a worm will turn.
지렁이도 밟으면 꿈틀한다.

42. Even Homer (sometimes) nods.
원숭이도 나무에서 떨어진다.

43. Every cloud has a silver lining. 전화위복

44. Every dog has his day.
쥐구멍에도 볕들 날 있다.

45. Every Jack has his jill. 헌 짚신도 짝이 있다.

46. Every minute seems like a thousand. 일각이 여삼추

47. Everyone has a skeleton in his closet.
털어서 먼지 안 나는 사람 없다.

48. Face the music. 울며 겨자 먹기

49. Fight fire with fire. 이열치열

50. Finders keepers, losers weepers. 줍는 사람이 임자다.

51. Fools rush in where angels fear to tread.
하룻강아지 범 무서운 줄 모른다.

52. Fortune knocks three times at everyone's door.
모든 사람에게 생애 세 번의 기회는 오게 마련이다.

53. Go home and kick the dog.
종로에서 빰 맞고 한강 가서 눈 흘긴다.

54. Greed has no limits.
말 타면 경마 잡히고 싶다.

55. Happiness and misery are not fated but self-sought.
행복과 불행은 운명 지워진 것이 아니라 스스로 이룩하는 것이다.

56. He bit off more than he can chew.
송충이는 솔잎을 먹어야 한다.

57. He got what he bargained for. 자업자득

58. He that will steal a pin will steal an ox.
바늘 도둑이 소도둑 된다.

59. Heaven helps those who help themselves.
하늘은 스스로 돕는 자를 돕는다.

60. He who makes no mistakes makes nothing.
실수를 하지 않는 사람은 아무 일도 못한다.

61. History repeats itself. By searching the old, learn the new.
온고이지신

62. Hunger is the best sauce. I'm so hungry I could eat a horse.
A good appetite is a good sauce.
시장이 반찬이다.

63. Icing on the cake. 금상첨화

64. If at first you don't succeed, try, try again. 칠전팔기

65. If it were a snake, it would bite you. 업은 아기 삼 년 찾는다.

66. Ignorance is bliss. 모르는 게 약이다.

67. I'll eat my hat. 내 손톱에 장을 지지겠다.

68. In one ear and out the other. 한 귀로 듣고 한 귀로 흘린다.
69. It is not until we lose health that we realize the value of it.
    건강을 잃고서야 비로소 건강의 소중함을 안다.
70. It's a piece of cake. 누워 떡 먹기
71. It's no use crying over spilt milk. 엎질러진 물이다.
72. It' takes two to tango. 두 손뼉이 맞아야 소리가 난다.
73. Kill two birds with one stone. 일석이조
74. Knock at the door and it will be opened.
    두드려라 그러면 열릴 것이다.
75. Let sleeping dogs lie. 긁어 부스럼/ 잠자는 사자를 건드리지 마라.
76. Let's get to the point. 거두절미
77. Life is full of ups and downs. 양지가 음지 되고 음지가 양지된다.
78. Like father, like son. 부전자전
79. Little drops of water make the mighty ocean.
    티끌 모아 태산
80. Look before you leap. 돌다리도 두드려 보고 건너라.
81. Love me, love my dog. 아내가 귀여우면 처갓집 말뚝보고 절한다.
82. Making a mountain out of a molehill. 침소봉대
83. Many hands make light work.
    백짓장도 맞들면 낫다.
84. Men always want to be a woman's first love, but women like to be a man's last romance.
    남자는 자신이 여자에게 첫 사랑이길 바라고 여자는 자신이 남자가 마지막으로 선택한 여자이길 바란다.
85. Match made in heaven. 천생연분
86. Mend the barn after the horse is stolen. 소 잃고 외양간 고친다.
87. Naked came we into the world and naked shall we depart from it.
    공수래공수거

88. Near neighbor is better than a distant cousin. 이웃사촌

89. Necessity is the mother of invention. 궁하면 통한다.

90. Never put off till tomorrow what can be done today.
오늘 할 일을 내일로 미루지 말라.

91. No news is good news. 무소식이 희소식

92. No one is too old to learn. 배움에는 나이가 없다.

93. No one spits on money. 돈에 침 뱉는 놈 없다.

94. Nothing ventured, nothing gained.
호랑이 굴에 들어가야 호랑이를 잡는다.

95. Once a beggar, always a beggar.
거지노릇 3일만 하면 그만두지 못한다.

96. Once bitten, twice shy.
자라보고 놀란 가슴 솥뚜껑보고 놀란다.

97. One man sows and another man reaps.
재주는 곰이 넘고 돈은 되놈이 번다.

98. One picture is worth a thousand words. Seeing is believing.
백문이 불여일견

99. One rotten apple spoils the barrel.
미꾸라지 한 마리가 온 웅덩이를 흐린다.

100. Out of the frying pan into the fire. 갈수록 태산

101. Pie in the sky. 그림의 떡

102 Rome wasn't built in a day.
첫술에 배부르랴./로마는 하루에 이루어진 것이 아니다.

103. Running around like a chicken with its head cut off.
호떡집에 불났다.

104. Searching for a needle in a haystack.
잔디밭에서 바늘 찾기

105. Self-help is the best help. 자조가 최선의 도움이다.

106. Slow and steady wins the race.
천리 길도 한 걸음부터

107. Sour grapes. 못 먹는 감 찔러나 본다.

108. Spare the rod and spoil the child.
회초리를 아끼면 아이를 버린다./자식이 귀엽거든 때려서 길들여라.

109. Speak of the devil. 호랑이도 제 말하면 온다.

110. Stabbed in the back. 믿는 도끼에 발등 찍힌다.

111. Stands out in the crowd. 군계일학

112. Starts off with a bang and ends with a whimper. 용두사미

113. Strike while the iron is hot. 쇠뿔은 단김에 빼라.

114. Sweet talk. 감언이설

115. Talking to the wall. There is none so blind. Water off a duck's back.
쇠귀에 경 읽기

116. That's easier said than done. 말은 행동보다 쉽다.

117. The cat that ate the canary. 눈감고 아웅 한다.

118. The cobbler's children go barefoot. 대장간에 식칼이 없다.

119. The end justifies the means. 모로 가도 서울만 가면 된다.

120. The fish that got away. 놓친 고기가 더 크다.

121. The good die young. 곧은 나무 먼저 찍힌다.

122. The grass is greener on the other side of the fence.
남의 떡이 커 보인다.

123. The pot calls the kettle black.
똥 묻은 개가 겨 묻은 개 나무란다.

124. The sparrow near a school sings the primer.
서당 개 삼 년에 풍월 한다.

125. The squeaky wheel gets the grease.
우는 아이 젖 준다.

126. The wise have long ears and a short tongue.
현명한 자는 남의 말을 많이 듣고 자기 말은 적게 한다.

127. The worst wheel of the cart always creaks most.
빈 수레가 요란하다.

128. There is no rule but has exceptions.
 예외 없는 규칙은 없다.

129. They're a storybook couple.
 깨가 쏟아진다.

130. Thick-skinned. 철면피

131. Thinking of other's advantage will turn out to one's own.
 타인의 이익을 생각해 주는 것이 곧 자신의 이익을 생각하는 것이다.

132. Thorn in the side. 눈에 가시

133. Thrown away like an old shoe. 헌 신짝 버리듯

134. Time is flying never to return.
 시간은 한번 가면 다시는 돌아오지 않는다.

135. Time heals all wounds. 세월이 약이라.

136. To each his own. 십인십색

137. To have the right chemistry. 이심전심

138. To have the upper hand. 배부른 흥정

139. To know a man is not to know his face, but to know his heart.
 사람을 안다는 것은 그의 얼굴을 아는 것이 아니라 그의 마음을 아는 것이다.

140. Tomorrow is a new day. Tomorrow is another day.
 내일은 내일이다.

141. Too many cooks spoil the broth.
 사공이 많으면 배가 산으로 올라간다.

142. To teach a fish how to swim.
 공자 앞에서 문자 쓴다.

143. Turning green with envy.
 사촌이 땅을 사면 배가 아프다.

144. Walls have ears.
 낮말은 새가 듣고 밤 말은 쥐가 듣는다.

145. We learn wisdom from failure much more than success.
 지혜는 성공했을 때보다 실패했을 때 더 많이 얻게 된다.

146. Well begun, half done.

시작이 반이다.

147. What's learned in the cradle is carried to the grave.
세 살 버릇 여든까지 간다.

148. What she doesn't know won't hurt her.
모르는 게 약이다.

149. When in Rome do as the Romans do.
로마에서는 로마의 풍속을 따르라.

150. When the cat's away, the mice will play.
범 없는 골에는 토끼가 스승이라.

151. Where there is a will, there is a way.
뜻이 있는 곳에 길이 있다.

152. Where there's smoke, there's fire.
아니 땐 굴뚝에 연기 날까

153. Within a stone's throw. 엎디면 코 닿을 데

154. Women and weather are not to be trusted.
여자와 날씨는 믿을 것이 못된다.

155. Worry wart. 걱정도 팔자

156. You can lead a horse to the water, but you cannot make him drink it.
말을 물 있는 곳으로 끌고 갈 수는 있어도 물을 마시게 할 수는 없다.

157. You could sell him the Brooklyn Bridge.
팥으로 메주를 쑨다 해도 믿는다.

158. You don't know what you've got until you've lost it.
구관이 명관

159. You have to make hay while the sun shines.
좋은 기회를 놓치지 마라.

160. You've cried wolf too many times.
콩으로 메주를 쑨다 해도 믿지 않는다.

161. You can lead a horse to water, but you can't make him drink.
평양감사도 자기 싫으면 그만

■(1~2) 다음에서 밑줄 친 부분의 의미와 가장 가까운 한국 속담은? (명지대 편입)

1. Don't just take my word for it, but try it yourself, After all the proof of <u>the pudding is in the eating</u>

   ① 백문이 불여일견　　② 일각이 여삼추
   ③ 금강산도 식후경　　④ 내 코가 석자

---

the proof of the pudding is in the eating(백문이 불여일견)
Every minute seems like a thousand.(일각이 여삼추)
A loaf of bread is better than the song of many birds.
= pudding rather than praise(금강산도 식후경)

2. I can't believe Tom turned down the promotion. You can lead a horse to water, but you can't make him drink.

   ① 목마른 놈이 우물을 판다.
   ② 얌전한 고양이가 부뚜막에 먼저 올라간다.
   ③ 못 오를 나무 쳐다보지도 말라
   ④ 평양감사도 자기 싫으면 그만.

You can lead a horse to water, but you can't make him drink.(평양감사도 자기 싫으면 그만.)–나는 톰이 승진을 거부했다는 것을 믿을 수 없다. 당신은 말을 물가에 데려 갈 수는 있어도, 물을 먹게 할 수는 없다.

3. 밑줄 친 곳에 가장 알맞은 영어 속담은? (행정 9급)

> The old saying "____________ " is never more true than when at the dinner table. In some parts of Korea, it is a sign of appreciation to drink one's tea or soup with much gusto and smacking of lips. But in most Western countries no noise should be made while eating. Eating utensils, too, differ from country to country.

① When in Rome, do as the Romans do

② All roads lead to Rome.

③ Habit is a second nature.

④ Every dog has its own day.

When in Rome, do as the Romans do. (로마에서는 로마의 풍속을 따르라)
All roads lead to Rome. (모든 길은 로마로 통한다)
Habit is a second nature. (습관은 제2의 천성이다)
Every dog has its own day. (쥐구멍에도 볕들 날 있다)

"로마에 가면 로마인이 하는 대로 행동하라."는 옛 속담이 저녁 식사를 할 때만큼 잘 들어맞는 경우도 없을 것이다. 한국의 몇몇 지역에서는 입맛을 다시거나 쩝쩝 소리를 내면서 차나 국을 마시는 것은 감사의 표시가 된다. 그러나 대부분의 서구 국가에서는 음식을 먹을 때 어떤 소리도 내어서는 안 된다. 또한 식기들도 나라마다 다르다.

4. 밑줄 친 부분에 가장 알맞은 것은? (경찰)

He who laughs last laughs ______.

① best　　② fast

③ never　　④ least

최후에 웃는 자가 가장 잘 웃는다.

1. ① 2. ④ 3. ① 4. ①

✻저|자|소|개

■ **배 상 정**

· 경희대학교 대학원 관광학 박사수료

현) 전북과학대학 호텔관광계열 교수(영문학박사)

[저 서]

· College English Conversation – 백산출판사

· 관광영어회화 – 백산출판사

· New Current English – 학문출판

· COLLEGE TOEIC – 백산출판사

· 호텔경영의 이해 – 대왕사(공저)

[논 문]

· 영문 관광표지 및 안내판의 개선 안에 관한 연구 외 다수

관광 · 호텔 · 항공 실무영어

2011년 2월 15일 초 판 발행
2023년 2월 28일 1판 3쇄 발행

저 자 배 상 정
발행인 한 인 환
발행처 도서출판 **기 문 사**
등 록 1978. 8. 9. NO. 6-0637
주 소 서울시 동대문구 안암로 50-1(용두동) 홍신빌딩 3층
전 화 02) 2265-7214/922-8662~8663
팩 스 02) 922-8772

homepage : www.kimoonsa.co.kr
e-mail : book@kimoonsa.co.kr

ISBN : 978-89-7723-486-4 93740

정가 : 20,000원